Byron

I. Lyric and Romance

by BERNARD BLACKSTONE

Published for the British Council
by Longman Group Ltd

Four shillings net (20p)

For a long period Byron has been regarded as a poet whose reputation stood higher among foreigners than in his own country: but in recent years the balance has been redressed, and it was no coincidence that in 1969 a tablet to his memory was unveiled in the Poets' Corner of Westminster Abbey, from which until then he had been excluded.

Byron was not only a prolific but a very diverse writer, and the full range of his work requires a more extended treatment than is possible in a single essay in the *Writers and Their Work* series. The present essay which replaces one written by Sir Herbert Read in 1951, discusses Byron's early lyrics, *Childe Harold*, the Oriental Tales and other narrative poems. It is the first of three studies of which the second, *Byron: Satiric, Reflective and Descriptive*, will deal with the verse satires, the journals and letters, and various poems, such as 'Darkness', 'The Dream', *The Prophecy of Dante*, and 'The Lament of Tasso'. The third, *Byron: Epic and Dramatic*, will include *Don Juan*, the dramas, and *The Island*. Each of these will include the biographical section which introduces the present essay.

Bernard Blackstone, the author of all three essays, was for nine years Byron Professor of English Literature at the University of Athens, during which period he was accorded the Freedom of the City of Missolonghi. He is now a Professor of English at the American University of Beirut, Lebanon. His published works include an edition of the papers of Nicholas Ferrar (1938), *English Blake* (1949), *The Consecrated Urn* (1959) and *The Lost Travellers* (1962).

BYRON

by

Bernard Blackstone

Edited by Ian Scott-Kilvert

BYRON

from a painting by THOMAS PHILLIPS
National Portrait Gallery

BYRON

I. LYRIC AND ROMANCE

by

BERNARD BLACKSTONE

PUBLISHED FOR
THE BRITISH COUNCIL
BY LONGMAN GROUP LTD

LONGMAN GROUP LTD
Longman House, Burnt Mill, Harlow, Essex

*Associated companies, branches and
representatives throughout the world*

First published 1970
© Bernard Blackstone 1970

Printed in Great Britain by
F. *Mildner & Sons, London, EC1*

CONTENTS

BYRON

I. INTRODUCTION

GEORGE GORDON, later to be the sixth Lord Byron, was
born in London on 22 January 1788 and died at
Missolonghi on 19 April 1824. His mother, Catherine
Gordon, was a Scottish heiress descended from the Stuarts;
his father, Captain John ('Mad Jack') Byron, nephew of the
fifth or 'wicked' Lord Byron and son of Admiral John
Byron (1723-1786) traced his long line of scapegrace
forebears back to the Ernegis and Radulfus de Burun who
had come over with William the Conqueror. A history
of violence runs through both the maternal and the paternal
line of Byron's family.

Captain John Byron's first marriage had been to the
Marchioness of Carmarthen after her divorce from the
Marquis in 1779; Byron's half-sister Augusta was the only
surviving child of this marriage. Whether or not Mad Jack
ill-treated his wife, as some said but Byron later denied ('It
is not by "brutality" that a young officer in the Guards seduces
and carries off a Marchioness, and marries two heiresses'),
she died in January 1784, and her £4,000 a year departed
with her; the Captain had to look round again. He met
Catherine Gordon of Bight, a girl of twenty with an estate
worth more than £23,000, at Bath, and married her in
May 1785. He rapidly ran through her fortune and de-
camped to France to avoid his creditors. He returned to
England in time for the birth of his son in 1788, but was
back in France by September 1790; whence he wrote to his
sister on 16 February 1791: 'With regard to Mrs Byron, I am
glad she writes to you. She is very amiable at a distance; but
I defy you and all the Apostles to live with her two months,
for, if any body could live with her, it was me . . . For my
son, I am happy to hear he is well; but for his walking, 'tis
impossible, as he is club-footed.' Captain Byron died on
2 August 1791.

The club-footed poet was brought up by his neurotic mother in Aberdeen, after their removal from London in 1789, in what used to be called 'straitened circumstances'. He had a lower-middle-class education at 'a School kept by a Mr *Bowers*, who was called "*Bodsy* Bowers" by reason of his dapperness. It was a School for both sexes. I learned little there, except to repeat by rote the first lesson of Monosyllables—"God made man, let us love him" . . . ' It is tempting to speculate what Byron's future might have been but for the cannon-ball which removed the fifth lord's grandson from the succession to the title in 1794. Lord Byron's own death at Newstead on 21 May 1798 meant George Gordon's accession to the peerage, to Newstead Abbey, and to the many debts incurred by the 'wicked lord'. Byron and his mother settled in at Newstead in August 1798.

There were three years of residence at Newstead, of neighbourly visits (Mary Chaworth, his first love, lived next door at Annesley Hall), of attendance at Dr Glennie's school in Dulwich. In 1801 came the removal to public school life at Harrow. In 1805 he went up to Trinity, Cambridge, where he did little work but made a number of friends and prepared his first volume of poems, *Hours of Idleness*, for the press. From this point onwards the incidents of his life are so closely interwoven with his writing that all I need give here is a skeleton survey, to be filled up in detail as we follow his career as a poet.

Hours of Idleness appeared in June 1807 and was contemptuously noticed by *The Edinburgh Review* of January 1808. 'As an author, I am cut to atoms by the E. Review', he wrote in a letter of 27 February; 'it is just out, and has completely demolished my little fabric of fame . . .' He replied with *English Bards and Scotch Reviewers* (March 1809), a brilliant and devastating satire; and set out (2 July 1809) for the Continent. He travelled through Portugal and Spain, Greece and Asia Minor, returning to Britain in July 1811 with the first two cantos of *Childe Harold* in his portmanteau.

Published in March 1812, the new poem had an immediate success: on the morrow of its appearance he notes, 'I awoke to find myself famous'. This extraordinary fame, greater perhaps than any other poet has enjoyed in his lifetime, endured to the end of his life and beyond. He became the idol of London high society, and his amours, particularly that with Lady Caroline Lamb, were notorious. *Childe Harold* was followed in the years from 1813 to 1816 by the succession of Oriental (and other) Tales, beginning with *The Giaour* (May 1813) and ending with *The Prisoner of Chillon* (Dec. 1816) which confirmed his standing as the foremost of European poets.

In 1809 he took his seat in the House of Lords, and on 27 February 1812 made his maiden speech, opposing a bill which specified the death penalty for frame breaking. On 2 January 1815 he married the blue-stocking heiress Annabella Milbanke. The marriage was not a happy one, and there were scandals about Byron's relationship with his half-sister Augusta and his homosexual tendencies; a daughter, Ada, was born in 1815, but in March 1816 a legal separation was agreed upon and in April Byron left England for ever.

Eight years of life remained to him. They were filled with feverish creative activity—the second part of *Childe Harold* (Canto III, published in November 1816, Canto IV, published in April 1818), the dramas, the enormous panorama of *Don Juan*. He formed the last and most important of his friendships, with Shelley; the first meeting was at Geneva in May 1816, and the acquaintance deepened as the two poets pursued their curious interlacing orbits through the length and breadth of Italy from 1818 to 1822.

The Italian years were filled with many adventures, but Byron's last real attachment of a heterosexual kind was to Teresa, the nineteen-year-old wife of the fifty-eight-year old Count Alessandro Guiccioli, who remained his mistress until his final journey to Greece. They met in Venice in 1819; the curious sexual *mores* of Italy at this period made it possible for Byron to reside in the Count's palace as

cavalier servente of the Countess ('What shall I do? I am in
love, and tired of promiscuous concubinage, and have now
an opportunity of settling for life.') There were difficulties,
however (it is possible to be too famous for comfort); the
legal separation of the Guicciolis, sojourn of Teresa under
her parental roof, reunion, quarrels over *Don Juan*, which
Teresa thought too cynical. The scene shifts from Venice
to Ravenna, from Ravenna to Pisa. Love is interspersed with
fights and with political plotting for the freedom of Italy,
saddened by the death of his illegitimate daughter Allegra.
'Awful work, this love', Byron comments ruefully in a
letter to Tom Moore of 19 September 1821.

But soon the awful work was to be over for ever. The
Greek war of independence, simmering for decades, broke
into open flame in 1821. Shelley wrote his stirring drama,
Hellas. English philhellenes formed a London Committee
for the promotion of the Greek cause. All eyes turned to
Byron, the greatest living philhellene, and when in 1822 he
was approached by the London Greek Committee he was
not slow to respond. In all his wanderings his heart and
mind had remained faithful to the land which, as he had
long ago declared, had 'made him a poet . . . a land it is a
privilege even to have visited'—which, when even its
memory passes for a moment across his page, lifts it 'into
sudden blaze', so that the mere recollection of 'those magical
and memorable abodes' (*Childe Harold* IV, Dedication) is
sufficient to fill his verse with subtlety and sweetness. Byron
sailed for Greece on 24 April 1823; after a stay in
Cephalonia, then a British protectorate, he arrived at
Missolonghi in January 1824. He died there of fever on
19 April 1824. His remains, which the Greeks wished to
inter in the Temple of Theseus in Athens, were transported
to England, refused a burial in Westminster Abbey, and
finally laid to rest by the side of the 'wicked lord' in the
family vault in Hucknall Torkard church. Perhaps his best
requiem was reported by the peasant poet John Clare, who
in his later madness fancied himself to be Byron and com-

posed a new *Childe Harold*. He is writing in his 1824
journal:

> I was wandering up Oxford Street on my way to Mrs Emmerson's
> when my eye was suddenly arrested by straggling groups of the common
> people collected together & talking about a funeral I did as the rest did
> though I could not get hold of what funeral it could be but I knew it
> was not a common one by the curiosity that kept watch on every
> countenance. By & by the group collected into about a hundred or more
> when the train of a funeral suddenly appeared on which a young girl
> that stood beside me gave a deep sigh & uttered 'Poor Lord Byron'.

II. EARLY LYRICS

No one would wish to pin Byron's fame to his lyrics, and
least of all to the early ones, but this verse has certain virtues
which have been commonly overlooked. It is beautifully
controlled, civilized, articulate. Some of it is frigid, and one
cannot say worse of poetry than that. A lot of it is school-
boyish—as we should expect from a schoolboy; boyishly
bombastic, rhapsodical, eager to make an effect; yet with a
subtle turn of irony, even of ambiguity. We are not always
sure how to take it. Satire is already present, though it is
filtered out as the various editions appear (*Fugitive Pieces*,
1806; *Poems on Various Occasions*, 1807; *Hours of Idleness*,
1807; *Poems Original and Translated*, 1808).

Hours of Idleness is *juvenilia*, but better *juvenilia* on the
whole than the early work of Wordsworth, Coleridge,
Shelley or Keats. Much of it is sentimental and unreal, but
it is not mushy as Coleridge and Shelley can be mushy, and
its dallying with the Gothic is less obsessed with charnel
horrors than are Wordsworth's and Shelley's excursions into
the same field. Blake's *Poetical Sketches* (1783) affords the
closest comparison, with a strikingly similar range of
subjects: Ossianic imitations, pastiches of Gray and Collins,
ballads and Gothic tales, prologues to plays, love songs.
Where Blake imitates Spenser, the Elizabethan lyric poets,

the Shakespearian drama, Byron gives us translations from
or paraphrases of the classics, together with verse epistles,
satirical pieces, meditations on time and death. Thomas
Moore's erotic poems are an obvious influence in many of
the love lyrics.

Hours of Idleness was devastatingly reviewed by Lord
Brougham in the famous *Edinburgh Review* critique of
January 1808, an attack which drew from Byron his even
more famous counter-blast of *English Bards and Scotch
Reviewers* in March of the following year. Brougham's
strictures were on the whole just, though severe—he hardly
allows for the poet's youth, nor sees any hope for his future
writing. It is odd that he and other reviewers missed the
impact of lines like these:

> And scatter flowers on the dust I love
> ('On the Death of a Young Lady')
> The yellow harvest's countless seed
> ('Imitated from Catullus')
> Where now the bats their wavering wings extend
> ('Elegy on Newstead Abbey')
> Gilds with faint beams the crystal dews of rain
> ('Childish Recollections')

I cite these not as Arnoldian touchstones, but as pointers to
that felicity of phrase which only major poets achieve, and
which Byron's 'lion paw' was to pat with such effortless
skill into the great stanzas of *Childe Harold* and *Don Juan*.

Significant as they are to a biographer or a student of
Byron's early emotional interests (including his ardent
schoolboy friendships, his love of sea and mountain, his
feeling for antiquity, his need for solitude) there is hardly
one of these lyrics which an anthologist of Byron would
judge indispensable. A possible exception is the stark
'Fragment', 'Hills of Annesley, bleak and barren', which
conveys the young poet's bitterness at his rejection by his
first love, Mary Chaworth—a sense of immedicable loss
which persisted throughout his life. Another kind of loss

permeates 'I would I were a careless child', where a certain *weltschmerz* already appears:

> Few are my years, and yet I feel
> The world was ne'er designed for me . . .

and *Childe Harold* (Canto III, lxix, Canto IV, clxxviii) is anticipated in

> Fain would I fly the haunts of men—
> I seek to shun, not hate mankind;
> My breast requires the sullen glen,
> Whose gloom may suit a darken'd mind.

This may strike us as exaggerated, but it is not derivative as are so many of the other *Idleness* poems: a personality is already emerging. So too are certain 'correlatives' (images, external equivalents to psychic states) such as the cave, the mountain's craggy side, Ocean's wildest roar; and the self-searching pathos of

> Though pleasure stirs the maddening soul,
> The heart—the heart—is lonely still

projects the perennial Byron.

Other lyrics of the pre-Continental period (i.e. before 1809), given the title of *Occasional Pieces* by Byron's first editors, offer a greater variety of tone. Some show a shrewd appreciation of human—and especially feminine—weaknesses, as 'To a Vain Lady' (1807), 'To Anne' (1807) and 'When we two parted' (1808); the latter (which does figure in all the anthologies) is interesting as a metrical experiment: dimeters are rare in English verse, and anapaestic dimeters even rarer: Byron manages his with considerable skill. This is a point worth making, I think, as Byron has never received his due as a prosodist. The 'Lines Inscribed Upon a Cup Formed From a Skull' is a complex poem which raises a theme Byron was to exploit more fully in *Childe Harold* (see below, p. 22). 'Inscription on the Monument of a Newfoundland Dog' introduces Byron the animal-lover, the collector of cats, peacocks, bears, geese, wolves, of whom I shall have more to say in a later essay. We must note, finally, an early statement of the Lost Paradise theme in 'To a Lady, on Being Asked my Reason for Quitting England in the Spring' (2 Dec. 1808).

III. *CHILDE HAROLD'S PILGRIMAGE*

As every schoolboy knows, Byron woke on a March morning in 1812 to find himself famous. Without knowing it (for he valued far more the satire, 'Hints from Horace', which he had also brought back with him from his Near Eastern tour) he had written the work which England (and still more Europe) had been waiting for. At once it was recognized that a poet of major stature had arisen. With *Childe Harold* 'la brumeuse Albion' ceased to be a mere nation of shopkeepers and was projected on the literary screen of Europe.

Childe Harold is the mirror of Europe and the Mediterranean world, a concave mirror focusing past and present, observation and reflection, nature and art and the life of man in a vast synthesis. Or we may see it as a net thrown over Europe and the Near East, reticulating space and time and that which is beyond both: indeed the marvellous line in the Coliseum passage of Canto IV,

When the stars twinkle through the loops of time (cxliv)

might stand as the motto of the *Pilgrimage* as a whole, taking 'loops of time' to mean not simply the loops or rents made by time in the structure of the amphitheatre, but gaps in time itself, fissures permitting a penetration of past into present, and of eternity into time.

There are other consonances, linking the elements. That Byron was the most 'elemental' of the Romantics was clear to his early commentators, including the greatest of them, Matthew Arnold, with his 'fount of fiery life' ('Memorial Verses', 6-14); what does not seem to have been noted by any of his critics is that *Childe Harold* is a work with an elemental structure, and that this structure may be called Heracleitan. The key to the whole poem lies in Heracleitus' *On the Universe*, XXV: 'Fire lives the death of air, and air lives the death of fire; water lives the death of earth, earth that of water'. This means that the poem has a cyclic structure, more complicated than the Heracleitan formula itself suggests. Thus in Canto I—a curiously 'land-locked' canto, in view of its peninsular contours—the dominant elements are earth and fire; these 'die' into the earth and water of Canto II, which 'dies' in its turn into the fire and water of Canto III. Canto IV is pre-eminently the celebration, in Rilke's sense of the word, of water and air, but as the culminating canto it gathers up fire and earth into airy and liquid patterns of art and architecture hitherto un-attempted. These points will become clearer as we survey the cantos in turn, though their full implications cannot of course be presented within the limits of an essay as short as this. Nor, for that matter, can the strange congruence of *Childe Harold* with that other quadripartite masterpiece, T. S. Eliot's *Four Quartets*, which is as *consciously* patterned on Heracleitus as Byron's poem is *unconsciously* and, one might say, instinctively. Both works mediate 'this grace dissolved in place' ('Marina', 16), 'The point of intersection of the timeless / With time' ('The Dry Salvages', v, 18, 19) at certain climactic loci, 'places which also are the world's end' ('Little Gidding', I, 35, 36). It is odd that Eliot, who has done something to reinstate Byron, should have turned a cold shoulder on *Childe Harold*.

But it is time to look at the separate cantos. In Canto I, after the opening stanzas of departure and voyaging, we leave the sea and, except for a brief allusion to Tagus (xiv) and to other streams as boundaries (xxxiii, xxxiv), we quit the watery element in general. Byron concentrates on the earth as mother, fruit-bearing and sustaining, ceaselessly and uncomplainingly restoring man's depredations (a theme to be taken up again in Canto III), and on fire in its destructive mask of war (xlvii). Nature's bounty is contrasted with man's ignorant self-slaughter (xlvii) and impiety—Byron's *lacrimae rerum* is Virgilian here, the Virgil of the *Eclogues* and the *Georgics*:

> Oh, Christ! it is a goodly sight to see
> What heaven has done for this delicious land:
> What fruits of fragrance blush on every tree!
> What goodly prospects o'er the hills expand!
> But man would mar them with an impious hand . . . (I, xv)

—and the intensity of his concern fuses history and insight in the first of his great dramatic ideograms, the figure of War:

> Lo! where the Giant on the mountain stands,
> His blood-red tresses deep'ning in the sun,
> With death-shot glowing in his fiery hands,
> And eye that scorcheth all it glares upon . . . (I, xxxix)

Canto I, land-locked and earth-bound, lacks a dimension of enthusiasm, of affection as distinguished from concern, which enters the scene only with the Pilgrim's entry into Greek seas in Canto II. In the first canto Byron is the observer, sympathetic but somewhat detached; delighting in all that is new and strange, but at the same time unable to shake off a mask of adolescent cynicism and boyish bravado. This speaks in the opening stanza, with its anti-invocation: is the poem to be 'romantic' or satiric? We cannot tell. The uncertainty of tone persists through the canto, and finds a stylistic correlative in the feeble Spenserianisms—'Whilome', 'hight', 'mote be', and so on—which go a long way to rob the narrative of the immediacy it otherwise possesses.

But the characteristic Byronic virtues are not long in manifesting themselves. Even in the *juvenilia* we noted his power of condensing a world of meaning into a single phrase and here it is again:

And Mammon wins his way where Seraphs might despair (I, ix)

And traverse Paynim[1] shores, and pass Earth's central line (I, xi)

And Tagus dashing onward to the deep,
His fabled golden tribute bent to pay (I, xiv)

Swept into wrecks anon by Time's ungentle tide! (I, xxiii)

and, most superb, and perhaps Byron's own unconscious epitaph: 'By all forgotten, save the lonely breast' (I, xci). This has the taut resonance of 'Among thy mightier offerings here are mine!', a line which Arnold appends as the motto, as it were, of his Golden Treasury *Poetry of Byron*. And it is worth noting how many of Byron's greatest lines are monosyllabic, how economical are the means employed by this supposedly rhetorical poet to achieve his effects:

When the stars twinkle through the loops of time (IV, cxliv)

I turn'd from all she brought to those she could not bring
(III, xxx)

And Ardennes waves above them her green leaves (III, xxvii)

—the list is interminable. It is worth noting too how many of these are ideograms:

I stood in Venice, on the Bridge of Sighs (IV, i)

There is a stern round tower of other days (IV, xcix)

There is a tomb in Arqua;—rear'd in air ... (IV, xxx)

This kind of genius, like Shakespeare's, disdains the aid of magniloquence in its highest flights.

By 'ideograms' in Byron I mean crystallizations, or projections outward in images or weighted phrases of a total situation. These are more than figures of speech—similes, metaphors, personifications—and more than epigrams, neat capsules focusing a meaning. Byron thought, or thought-

[1] pagan.

felt, in ideograms, when he was working at his intensest. He
is the least conceptual of our poets, and in that sense the
least 'reflective'. The ideogram is the product of a fusion of
Byron with his environment, and by 'environment' I mean
what is there at the time no matter whether the 'what' is
material—sea, Doric column, Turkish tomb-stone, Venetian
palace; or immaterial—recollections of the past, resent-
ments, sentimental sense-data (scents, tastes, etc.): all are
felt as projections of an inner situation, in indivisible union
with it, so that 'inner' and 'outer' are no longer antitheses,
but co-exist in the artistic construct, and only there. 'You
are the music, while the music lasts.' This was Byron's *real*
dramatization, and not the chamber-dramas of 1816
(*Manfred*) to 1822 (*Werner*) which constitute, to my mind,
somewhat unresonant projections in active terms of the
main ideograms which establish themselves, as we shall see,
in the course of *Childe Harold* and its coda, the Oriental
Tales. Byron's imagination is handicapped the moment
it separates from its spatio-temporal ground; he has to
feel himself living, vibrating in the moment before he can
begin to react, to adjust himself as a sea-creature adapts
itself to the new densities, saltiness, anfractuosities of the
pool into which the latest tide has swept it.

I am tempted to linger over Canto I, a part of the total
œuvre which has never been accorded its deserts, but I have
no space here to do more than point to some outstanding
features. The *elemental* character of the whole poem is
established at the outset: it is 'to the elements' that the
Childe 'pour'd his last Good Night' (xiii): *to* the elements,
not simply amid the elements or making use of them for
theme or variation; a relationship is at once suggested. In the
'Welcome, ye deserts, and ye caves!' of the concluding
stanza of the 'Good Night' itself (an important early lyric)
we pass definitively into that strange world of the 'lost
travellers' which I have tried to describe in my book of that
title. Here the wanderer finds himself (in the twofold meaning of the phrase) in a context of elemental entities pre-

senting their duple aspects of welcome and menace; man is restored to his pre-civilized status of simple earth-dweller, of 'stranger and pilgrim'. Together with this restored primitivity comes a new relationship of understanding and 'empathy' with the non-human creation. The brilliant stanzas on the bullfight (lxxii-lxxx) are more than a virtuoso performance: their dual ethos of delight in energy and pity for suffering point on to the field of Waterloo in Canto III, and the dying gladiator in Canto IV. The adjectives I have just used: twofold, duple, dual, are meant to stress the contrapuntal relationship of the poet to his theme.

Canto II brings Greece and self-discovery: the texture of the verse knits together, the scattered observations of Canto I are replaced by a focused vision, the great ideograms emerge and establish themselves in terms of shattered pediment and broken column, of light Greek and grave Moslem, of lonely cypress and sunlit bay. Byron has found his world. And from now on, though he was not to see Greece again until the sacrificial journey of 1823, this was to remain Byron's world; Regency London, Switzerland, Italy are experienced and unconsciously judged in the perspective of this land which, as he said, had made him a poet.

It had made him too, in some sense, a philosopher. Greece forced Byron to reflect, and from Canto II onward the element of reflection rather than satiric comment enters as a fourth dimension (along with history, topography and personal feeling) into the texture of the poem. No one seems to have noted that *Childe Harold* is the product of an English public-school education, elementary though such an observation is once it is made. But for the grind at Greek and Latin we should have no *Childe Harold*: it was all very well for Byron to wave Horace away—'Then farewell Horace, whom I hated so'—in Canto IV; you just cannot wave Horace away, once you have been exposed to him; he is there for the rest of your life, as are Virgil and Homer,

Aeschylus and Plato, and the ancient world won and lost
at Actium, and

> the barren spot
> Where sad Penelope o'erlook'd the wave (II, xxxix)

As the Greek light penetrated the stones, that marvellous
dry light that isolates as it connects, so too it entered Byron's
storehouse of mental bric-à-brac, disinfecting here, cauteriz-
ing there, putting paid to a number of psychic accounts,
stimulating new energic currents. 'So this is what it was all
about!', we can imagine him saying, his thoughts going
back to Harrow and Cambridge as he stood among the
fallen columns of the Temple of Olympian Jove on that
Christmas Day of 1809.

Coming to Athens from the north-west, via Cephalonia,
Patras, Ioannina, Tepelene, Missolonghi, Delphi, and Phyle,
he was to some extent prepared for what it had to offer.
But the special qualities of Attica are not anticipated in any
other region of Greece, and they impinged on Byron with
something of the force of a revelation. Behind the wretched-
ness of the Turkish village which sprawled around the
Acropolis he was moved to divine the 'dear city of
Cecrops'[1] and the groves of Plato and Aristotle; beyond
these his vision moved in ever-widening circles to
Marathon and Thermopylae and the islands. The chief
imagination of Europe had found its home and its theme.

The result is startling. Gothic mists, Spenserian
fantasies are swept away: Canto II opens with an im-
passioned but classically measured appeal to the goddess of
Wisdom to aid him in achieving the ultimate goal of self-
knowledge. Dwelling briefly on the prevalence of un-
wisdom in a commercial age (Byron's approach here is
very close to Blake's), he sweeps on to a dramatic contrast
between 'men who never felt the sacred glow' and those

---

[1] Quoted by Marcus Aurelius (*Meditations*, IV, 23) from an unknown
source.

'grand in soul' who were Athens' glory in old days:

> The warrior's weapon and the sophist's stole
> Are sought in vain, and o'er each mouldering tower,
> Dim with the mist of years, gray flits the shade of power. (II, ii)

Note the intense visualization here: it is not just a metaphor or a personification; here is the tower, in its crumbling immediacy, and here is the grey shadow, a visible if impalpable shape, 'flitting' like a bat between its pinnacles. This connective force, possessed by no other English poet except Shakespeare, informs the whole of the *Pilgrimage* from now on. Reading this poetry, we must be ceaselessly alert. We cannot settle down into the repose which, for instance, Keats's verse invites for its full reception; a repose in which the Keatsian physiograms, densely encapsulated seeds of meaning, sink down into our muddy and fecund depths, to unfold in dark passages and to re-emerge as articulate wisdom. For Byron, the wisdom must be there from the beginning: he is a classical poet, living in bright air, the air of columns, theatres, temples brilliant in the sun. Wisdom is *there* if we can but seize it, a heritage from the past, something to be recovered, not remade. Keats works, to put it crudely, in terms of roots, Byron in terms of columns. We can come to terms with Byron only when we have come to terms with the past.

Canto II, then, is Byron's 'self-discovery' canto, and it is filled with this exhilarating sense of the new and the unexpected. It is bound together by the unifying power of the Greek sea which I shall have more to say about when I come to discuss the Oriental Tales. Seas and mountains are Byron's major emblems. Mountains are a bit stiff, a bit portentous: they do not *move*, and for Byron movement is life. They are very grand, and the Byronic scene could not get on without them, but they represent, in the inner panorama, aspiration rather than fulfilment. In a sense they are recalcitrant to Byron's imagination. He may, like the Prisoner of Chillon,

>   . . . bend
> Once more, upon the mountains high
> The quiet of a loving eye,   (330-1)

but do they *respond* to that love? Wordsworth did not want them to: he wanted the father-figure, rather stiff, rather remote, threatening, punishing, keeping him in order. Byron needed something different, he had already had enough of Captain Byron, and as for Mrs Byron, *that* mother-figure was *out*. The sea provided a marvellous complex fulfilling his needs on the figurative plane: masculine in its power, violence, authority; feminine in its beauty, languor, fecundity. In the Oriental Tales we do not know whether Zuleika, Leila and Medora are emblems of the sea or whether the sea is the totality of Medora, Leila and Zuleika. The mountain is barren, majestic, remote; identified to some extent with the hero himself, at least an ideal he can live up to, breathing its air of freedom (*Childe Harold*, II, lxxxvii), of release from the pettiness of sea-level concerns (this was a notion Byron bequeathed to Matthew Arnold), sharing its clinical, aseptic indifference. But never a father figure as with Wordsworth.

The opening stanzas of Canto II move through architectural symbolism (notice here how the skull image expands and contracts through the 'temple' metaphor from the 'enduring bone' of the human skeleton to the ruined columns among which Byron sits as he writes) to an indignant condemnation of Lord Elgin's depredations on the Parthenon (II, xi-xv). These stanzas are a sort of prologue to the 'action' of the poem, for stanza xvi brings us back to Harold, 'the gloomy wanderer', on his sea-borne way to the Hellenic shore. In a sense stanzas xvi-xix are a farewell to the purely descriptive side of *Childe Harold*. They give us a well-realized, bustling, extrovert view of life aboard ship; the detail is perfect, and interesting in its own right. But from now on there will be no more such objective descriptions. Greece changes all that. Greece introduces Byron to the new dimension of a time which is also eternity, of a space in which a terrible sun burns up the distinctions of *thine* and *mine*, of *here* and *there*, in which life is the shade cast by the olive tree, and survival the oil from its berries, stored up carefully against an 'unimaginable, zero' winter. For such winters also come, in these 'Edens of the eastern wave'.

The Greek vistas of Canto II are blended of earth and water: air exists as an abstract, as the medium through which actuality is viewed, not as a part of that actuality itself, since 'air' for Byron is freedom. Air enters into the Venetian scene of the fourth canto, though Venice too is enslaved, through the powers of art, through music and through painting and architecture and sculpture in a sense *as* music, and thus exists in its own right together with 'the wat'ry floor' as the double paradigm: air/water on which the great ideograms of Canto IV are to be built. In Canto II, however, air is stressed only once, in the ironic paradox of the Hymettan bee, 'the free-born wanderer of thy mountain air' flitting unconcerned over enslaved Athens. So too in the exordium to *The Giaour*: 'no breath of air' breaks the wave 'That rolls below the Athenian's grave'. The great artefacts of Venice mock her Austrian oppressors and in this sense are invulnerable, like the ghost of Hamlet's father, 'like the air': Byron did not anticipate modern bombing. But in Greece 'fire' has died into 'earth', 'air' has died into 'water'. The indifference of the Giaour to the beauty of his surroundings is the necessary indifference of air and fire (cf. Hotspur and the Dauphin in Shakespeare) to the elements they are to redeem (I return to this point in my discussion of the Oriental Tales). In Canto II and in *The Giaour, The Corsair, The Bride of Abydos* we are in a crumbling world: 'Nature still is fair', but for the Byronic humanism (again like Shakespeare's, and Blake's: 'Where man is not, Nature is barren') there is no completion outside the human-natural nexus. Byron is thoroughly eighteenth-century in seeing nature as a landscape *with* figures.

The figures in Canto II are unheroic. *The Giaour* was

to redeem this, to some extent, but the full redemption could only come with the personal commitment of 1823. The tyrannical Turks come out best: at least they have dignity: 'Unmoved the Moslem sits, the light Greek carols by' (x). Stanza xxvii introduces an archetypal figure, the monk of Athos, expressing Byron's love of solitary musing, and beyond that of his feeling for another kind of commitment, the total surrender to other-worldly values:

> More blest the life of godly eremite,
> Such as on lonely Athos may be seen,
> Watching at eve upon the giant height . . . (xxvii)

This is a figure muted in the later poems (*Lara*, *The Corsair*, *Manfred*) but potent, one feels, within Byron's imagination: one can imagine him, as one cannot imagine any other of the great Romantics, settling for orthodoxy and the monastic life—'as a refuge from insanity', to quote Blake again. Against the Monk is set, in some fascinatingly realistic-romantic stanzas (lv-lxvi), the grimly colourful Ali Pasha (whose actuality comes out even better in the letters he wrote at this time, to his mother and others):

> It is not that yon hoary lengthening beard
> Ill suits the passions that belong to youth . . .
> But crimes that scorn the tender voice of ruth,
> Beseeming all men ill, but most the man
> In years, have mark'd him with a tiger's tooth . . . (lxiii)

Nevertheless, there is a human immediacy in Canto II that we miss in the other three cantos. Greece brought him into relationship—with the Maid of Athens, Theresa Macri, with the Turkish girl whose adventure is celebrated in *The Giaour*, with a considerable group of Philhellenes in Athens. And also with a literature: Byron learned modern Greek and was sufficiently interested in its development to draw up some 'Remarks on the Romaic or Modern Greek Language', written in the spring of 1811, in which one may note Byron's attraction to Greek ballad poetry.

But of course what we remember of Canto II are the island or promontory vistas, where the powers of sea and earth—the dynamic and the static—intermingle; more than any other of the cantos this is the great hymn of the elements. And of the elements—unchanging, serene, benignly interpenetrating—in contrast to man, futilely bellicose, stupidly destructive. From stanza lxxxv to stanza xciii the great music flows, to merge at xcv with Byronic aplomb in the personal grief of his lament for the choirboy Edleston ('Thou too art gone, thou loved and lovely one!'), and end with the bitter acceptance of loneliness:

> What is the worst of woes that wait on age?
> What stamps the wrinkle deeper on the brow?
> To view each loved one blotted from life's page,
> And be alone on earth, as I am now.   (xcviii)

Between the second and the third cantos of *Childe Harold* came the return to England from the Near Eastern tour, the fame brought by the publication of the cantos then written (I and II), the death of Byron's mother and of many of his friends, the marriage with the heiress Annabella Milbanke, the failure of the marriage, the separation, and the exile. Canto III (published 1816) and Canto IV (1818) are the product of his second Continental sojourn, from which he never returned to England.

Much of Canto III expresses Byron's bitterness at his rejection by English society after the Annabella-Augusta scandal, and in this it is the most personal of the cantos, the sour first-fruits of exile. Indignation gives his verse a vehement and fiery quality; travel again becomes an escape, as in Canto I, and intensity of emotion fuses 'the wandering outlaw of his own dark mind' (iii) with the scenes through which he passes. Most critics have felt this greater unity of Cantos III and IV. When the expression of the emotion is simply melodic, however, as in the notorious 'that curse shall be Forgiveness' passage (IV, cxxxiii–cxxxvii), we are

conscious of strain and melodrama, we miss the correlatives
—desert, caves, wind and cloud—which give the very
similar outburst in Canto III, iii–v, its resonance.

The most common of all Byron's correlatives in Canto III
is fire—around this nucleus he constructs ideograms ex-
pressive of a wide variety of states of mind. Fire indeed is
of the essence of the creative mind itself, as he declares
openly at the outset of the canto:

> I *have* thought
> Too long and darkly, till my brain became,
> In its own eddy boiling and o'erwrought,
> A whirling gulf of phantasy and flame . . . (vii)

Fire in Canto III is to be both source and material; the fluid
rhythms of the Greek canto are replaced by passionate
personal stresses, rendering untenable the role of detached
observer he had sometimes assumed in the earlier cantos.
Indeed, from this point onwards it is useless to attempt to
distinguish between Byron and Childe Harold. It is Byron
himself who, after years of youthful dissipation has drunk
'from a purer fount, on holier ground' (in marrying
Annabella) 'And deem'd its spring perpetual; but in vain!'
(ix); it is Byron who now 'once more within the vortex,
roll'd /On with the giddy circle, chasing Time' (xi).

No wonder then that the first scene of the canto is
Byron's grimmest evocation of war, the field of Waterloo
(xvii–xxxiii). The connection with 'the giddy circle' is convincingly made through the ball at Brussels on the eve of
the battle,

> when Youth and Pleasure meet
> To chase the glowing Hours with flying feet   (xxii)

and the 'glow' of love is refashioned into a 'fiery mass / Of
living valour, rolling on the foe / And burning with high
hope', soon to 'moulder cold and low'. Counterpointed
with man's 'fiery' stupidities are the cool benisons of Nature,

proffered in vain (xxvii—see earlier, p. 15), and her in-
cessant efforts to restore the felicity man so wantonly
destroys:

> But when I stood beneath the fresh green tree,
> Which living waves where thou didst cease to live,
> And saw around me the wide field revive
> With fruits and fertile promise, and the Spring
> Come forth her work of gladness to contrive,
> With all her reckless birds upon the wing,
> I turn'd from all she brought to those she could not
>   bring. (xxx)

The pathos of this rapidly modulates into the gloomy
reflections on human life (xxxiv-xlv) which centre round
the antithetical figure of Napoleon—extreme in both
grandeur and misery. Byron opens the passage with an
acute observation, anticipating Freud, on the death wish:

> There is a very life in our despair,
> Vitality of poison . . . (xxxiv)

then sketches in the Emperor's character (with traits which
seem to draw somewhat on the Byronic hero), and closes
with an analysis, still in terms of fire, of the class of men of
which Napoleon is one:

> But quiet to quick bosoms is a hell,
> And *there* hath been thy bane; there is a fire
> And motion of the soul which will not dwell
> In its own narrow being . . . (xlii)

Turning once more from human folly to the calm of
Nature, Byron begins his voyage up the Rhine. Here he
cannot but be conscious of the river's antithetic history of
bloodshed, of warring barons and the softer annals of
chivalrous love, 'But still their flame was fierceness . . .'
(xlix); and his personal history of love and strife recurs
bitterly to his mind (lii-lv). He remembers his child Ada,

and his half-sister Augusta, to whom the stirring lyric 'The castled crag of Drachenfels' is inscribed. The martial grandeur of Drachenfels frowning down upon the gently flowing Rhine and the banks where

> peasant girls, with deep blue eyes,
> And hands which offer early flowers,
> Walk smiling o'er this paradise

is one of those antithetic ideograms in which Byron delighted. His verse habitually progresses by means of such contrasts—alternations from fierceness to tenderness, from grave to gay, from man to nature, from personal to impersonal. These antitheses function within the broader pattern of alternate descriptive, meditative, and confessional poetry which gives *Childe Harold* its uniqueness. There is a constant retraction and expansion of vistas from an intensely concentrated core, or 'nucleus', outwards in widening circles of descriptive and reflective data (often antithetical among themselves), and back again to 'the lonely breast'.

The lonely breast was not so lonely as the poem would lead us to believe, for Byron was accompanied by his doctor, Polidori, and was later joined at Geneva by his old travelling companion Hobhouse. Moreover it was at Geneva that he met Shelley and Mary Godwin on 27 May 1816, the day after his arrival. So began one of the decisive literary friendships. Shelley's influence on Byron is apparent in the increasingly 'metaphysical' note in his poetry from now on—and particularly in his nature descriptions. Shelley's admiration for Wordsworth led Byron to re-read him, and though I have never been able to see anything Wordsworthian in Byron's view of Nature, there are some undoubted echoes of phrase. On the whole however this steeping in Shelley's and Wordsworth's Nature-mystique helped Byron to the development of his own integrated vision.

Byron's 'Is it not better, then, to be alone / And love Earth only for its earthly sake?' (III, lxxi) seems a counterblast to

Wordsworthian metaphysics. Byron loved to merge himself in Nature—'I become / Portion of that around me, and to me / High mountains are a feeling . . .' (lxxii)—rather than to brood over her and philosophize as a 'spectator ab extra' (Coleridge's phrase for Wordsworth). What for Wordsworth is 'a motion and a spirit, that impels / All thinking things, all objects of all thought' ('Tintern Abbey') is for Byron a shared *life* in which he is caught up, which lives itself through him: concentration, rather than diffusion or 'interfusion':

> From the high host
> Of stars, to the lull'd lake and mountain-coast,
> All is concenter'd in a life intense,
> Where not a beam, nor air, nor leaf is lost . . . (lxxxix)

—a conception very close to Blake's

> For every thing exists and not one sigh nor smile nor tear,
> One hair nor particle of dust, not one can pass away.
> (*Jerusalem*, pl. 13, 66; pl. 14, 1)

More than this, it is clear that for Byron Nature makes psychic states and human situations concrete: it is not a question of the landscape being a mere stage on which this or that action may be presented: the action and the characters emerge from the landscape, which has held them *in potentia*. In a long note to stanza c of this canto Byron asserts the 'peculiar adaptation' of the scenery around Clarens[1] 'to the persons and events with which it has been peopled' by Rousseau; and, more than that, 'If Rousseau had never written, nor lived, the same associations would not less have belonged to such scenes . . .':

But this is not all: the feeling with which all around Clarens . . . is invested, is of a still higher and more comprehensive order than the mere sympathy with individual passion; it is a sense of the existence of love in its most extended and sublime capacity, and of our own participation of its good and of its glory: it is the great principle of the

[1] The scene of Rousseau's famous novel *La Nouvelle Héloise*.

universe, which is there more condensed, but not less manifested; and of which, though knowing ourselves a part, we lose our individuality, and mingle in the beauty of the whole.

This conception of love as the great principle is very far from Wordsworth's 'Wisdom and Spirit of the Universe! / Thou Soul which art the Eternity of Thought!'. Byron did not distinguish human—and sexual—love from the love of God or of Nature, and there is a physical quality in his intercourse with Nature—take for instance his grapplings with the sea—which would have revolted that 'solemn and unsexual man'. 'And thus I am absorb'd, and this is life', he cries in stanza lxxiii. Wordsworth's 'It is the first mild day of March' does indeed celebrate 'love' as 'a universal birth' but the poem is strangely untypical, and the 'love' very different from Byron's.

Rousseau, for Byron, is emphatically the prophet of love (lxxvi-lxxx)—'One, whose dust was once all fire'—yet the basic paradox cannot be avoided, and in the last stanzas of the passage he is also the oracle of revolution and war—

> For then he was inspired, and from him came,
> As from the Pythian's mystic cave of yore,
> Those oracles which set the world in flame,
> Nor ceased to burn till kingdoms were no more . . . (lxxxi)

Love and war, creation and destruction are inextricably interwoven in Byron's verse, as we shall see more clearly when we come to look at his Oriental Tales and the dramas. This is the fire 'which burns before the ice-cap reigns', in Eliot's 'East Coker': and Canto III of *Childe Harold* moves constantly between these polar conflagrations.

But relief there must be, and this Byron finds in the coolness and quiet of the lake of Geneva, even preferring it to 'Torn ocean's roar' (lxxxv). In solitude, at evening on the lake, he can sense 'the feeling infinite' which 'purifies from self' (xc). Such a mood, however, cannot last for long with Byron, and as he gazes on the mountains which surround

the lake his mind reverts to the early Persian fire-worship-
pers (xci); the change of mood is reflected in a sudden storm,
of which we are given a very vivid description (xcii, xciii).
Here too Byron longs for fusion with the elements:

> let me be
> A sharer in thy fierce and far delight,
> A portion of the tempest and of thee!

and the love-theme returns him to Rousseau (xcix-civ).
From this, by another swing of the pendulum, he moves on
to two very different writers who are associated with
Geneva: Voltaire and Gibbon, scoffers and iconoclasts,
'gigantic minds' whose aim was 'Titan-like, on daring
doubts to pile / Thoughts which should call down thunder,
and the flame / Of Heaven' (cv). This is an early sounding
of that Promethean note, the theme of the rebel against
divine tyranny, which was to occupy many of the dramas.
Voltaire and Gibbon are skilfully differentiated: 'The one
[Voltaire] was fire and fickleness . . .' (cvi), while Gibbon

> deep and slow, exhausting thought,
> And hiving wisdom with each studious year,
> In meditation dwelt, with learning wrought,
> And shaped his weapon with an edge severe,
> Sapping a solemn creed with solemn sneer;
> The lord of irony . . .   (cvii)

Canto III ends as it had begun with the remembrance of
his infant daughter. He addresses her from the standpoint
of deepening solitude which has been the tenor of this
canto:

> I stood and stand alone—remember'd or forgot (cxii)

—and this vision of her reaches into the future, with a
slant closer to Eliot's 'Animula' than to Wordsworth's
'Immortality' Ode:

> . . . to watch
> Thy dawn of little joys, — to sit and see
> Almost thy very growth, — to view thee catch
> Knowledge of objects, — wonders yet to thee! (cxvi)

These are the pleasures of parenthood he is not to know; but he looks to the future to bring a posthumous communion:

> My voice shall with thy future visions blend
> And reach into thy heart, — when mine is cold . . . (cxv)

With Canto IV the vistas re-open. A sense of oppression grips the third canto, with its personal present enclosed in an historic present, its gulfs of fire, even its landscape—the narrow gorge of the Rhine, and the 'arrowy Rhone' opening out at last into a lake-scene penned in by mountains. Within the canto itself Byron looks ahead to his liberation:

> Italia! too, Italia! looking on thee,
> Full flashes on the soul the light of ages . . . (III, cx)

exactly as, in Canto I, he had anticipated in his Parnassus stanzas (anticipated in the poem's sequence, that is, for as we know they were written on the spot) his entrance into Greece (I, lx-lxii). Now once again a historic past interfuses with majestic spaces; it is not Greece, so a dimension is lost, but it is the ancient world, or its vestibule, and with what gusto Byron launches into it!

> I stood in Venice, on the Bridge of Sighs;
> A palace and a prison on each hand:
> I saw from out the wave her structures rise
> As from the stroke of the enchanter's wand:
> A thousand years their cloudy wings expand
> Around me, and a dying Glory smiles
> O'er the far times, when many a subject land
> Look'd to the winged Lion's marble piles,
> Where Venice sate in state, throned on her hundred isles! (IV, i)

Here everything appears 'at airy distance' (IV, ii), we are rescued from the Teutonic oppressiveness of Canto III into a marvellous texture of light and light-differentiated structures rising miraculously from the waves—the sense of creation, of newness, of wonder is strong. Is there another poem in our language which opens with anything approaching this vitality?

I have already suggested that Canto IV is pre-eminently the manifestation of air and water, of water blending with air as in Canto II it penetrated the 'heroic earth' of Greece. This 'airiness' of Canto IV emerges in the frequent references to music, to wind as music (e.g. cvi), to death as somehow reanimated by air (xxx, cxi), to the rainbow (lxxii) which unites water, air and light—but one could go on indefinitely. Venice's supremacy is seen as this blending (ii), and it is precisely because of this that her greatness cannot be utterly destroyed; even under an alien tyranny (iii), she stands as an ideogram of *these* elemental values.

Canto IV is the culmination of *Childe Harold* above all in its assertion of the inclusive ideogram of the city. We have come in an enormous curve from the fragmentary cities of Canto I, unresonant, isolated by war from the total human context (earth ringed like the scorpion by fire), via Greece's heroic earth, washed by compassionate seas but cityless and resonant only of the past, and via the stifled and war-racked plains of central Europe, where for Byron cities hardly exist, to these towered, lucid panoramas in which each city is a separate ideogram alive with human values. Indeed Canto IV is the most 'human' of the cantos in its deep concern for the human condition; this sounds in the tenderness of 'Nor yet forget how Venice once was dear' (iii)—an abstract tenderness fusing spectator, place and history.

Canto IV is, indeed, the most fugal of the cantos. Here landscape, human life, history, personal reflection, and art are interwoven with incredible dexterity. Art, which again Byron sees in terms of 'air'—Tasso's echoes (iii), the Venus de Medici (xlix), the temple of Clitumnus (lxviii), Trajan's column (cxi), the Coliseum (cxxviii)—and of 'music' (St Peter's is 'Vastness which grows—but grows to harmonize

— / All musical in its immensities', a 'haughty dome
which vies / In air with Earth's chief structures . . .'(clvi)),
enters Byron's verse for the first time, for Canto I gives us
nothing, and Canto II presents structures which, being
Greek, are conceived of in existential terms transcending
those of art, and which in any case have been so far ab-
sorbed into the landscape that they are no longer distinguish-
able from it; Canto III, passing through Gothic scenes, is
an architectural blank.

   That he sees art in sexual terms will come as no surprise,
after his love-and-nature assimilations in Canto III; person-
ally I find this tiresome, and the stanzas celebrating
the Uffizi and the Pitti palace galleries (xlix-liii) strike
me as the least successful of the canto, but I am quite
ready to think that this too is one of the irrational anti-
Byronic prejudices which later criticism will correct. Be
that as it may, there can be no doubt that Byron's interweaving in this canto of past and present, of the scene with
art's representation of the scene (iv-vi), adds a facet if not a
dimension. I suppose for most critics this is the greatest of
the cantos: certainly it is the most complex, but I continue
to prefer Canto II, where (i) Byron's cosmic perceptions
(if one can use such a term) are most involved and (ii) his
egotism is at a minimum. By 'cosmic perceptions' I mean
his sheer capacity for penetrating the life of a scene in its
relation to time and that which is out of time and reacting
to it from a centre which is also out of time, and yet related.
From this penetration the great ideograms arise. Cantos I
and II express Byron's slow, hesitant emergence from the
trauma of birth, of Edinburgh and Newstead; then came the
second trauma of Annabella, the formidable reaction which
is Canto III, and the continued though subsiding reaction
which is Canto IV, leading to the final affirmation.

   But of course this fourth canto *is* the canto of splendours;
and since Italy is for Byron the ancient world, it is not
divorced from the great root-themes of Canto II. They
nourish it, in fact; and though, in the end, Byron had to

respond to the gravitational pull of his motherland, these twigs and scions of Greece on a more Western shore, together with his growing fame, helped to sustain him. The anonymity of the gloomy wanderer of Canto II was gone, and with it his freedom of response; his liaison with Teresa Guiccioli signified his acceptance of a certain bondage, a certain rôle. This acceptance brought its advantages; Byron was free to take stock, to put down roots, to branch out here and there (the interest in art is an example) and laugh at himself, as in *Beppo*, as well as at society. The satiric mode returns. But the roots are in water rather than earth, the stasis cannot be permanent. Hence, I think, the emphasis on cities in this canto. Separated from Greece, where the sanctities are at their most elemental—the brilliance of light, the clarity of water, the starkness of mountain, the purity of air—Byron looks for, and finds, 'objective correlatives' to these elemental forces in the human constructs which best express them. One might define Italy as the projection of Greece in art. The projection, in the sense of the extended expression—the drawing-out of what was implicit in the Greek nucleus; or, indeed, of the interpenetration here of the present with the past, of modern man with his environment. Greece had been the great correlative of solitude: not of loneliness, which is the ethos of Canto III, for in Greece, even today, one cannot be alone, the landscape itself eliminates the human insufficiency, but one can be solitary, infinitely detached from oneself and from one's cares and obsessions. Byron understood this: I think it was what he meant by his use of the word 'privilege'.

So the cities of Canto IV are detached fibres of the solitary nerve. All are antithetical, of course: Venice, 'The revel of the earth, the masque of Italy' is the most miserable victim of the Austrian oppressor; Rome, steeped in 'The double night of ages and of her, / Night's daughter, Ignorance'; Florence,

> Where the Etrurian Athens claims and keeps
> A softer feeling for her fairy halls.

> Girt by her theatre of hills, she reaps
> Her corn, and wine, and oil, and Plenty leaps
> To laughing life, with her redundant horn . . .(xlviii)

is also the city where Dante and Boccaccio's bones do *not*
lie (lvii, lviii). Ferrara, with its 'wide and grass-grown
streets / Whose symmetry was not for solitude', is the
scene of Tasso's long imprisonment. 'One of the Ferrarese
asked me', Byron remarks in a letter, 'if I knew "Lord
Byron", an acquaintance of his, *now* at Naples. I told him
"No!" which was true both ways, for I knew not the
imposter; and, in the other, no one knows himself . . .' No
one knows himself: as the Pilgrimage nears its end, its goal
of self-knowledge grows ever more remote, more *diffused*—
what is this self one seeks to know? The self of Newstead?
of Athens? of London? of the Rhine? of here and now?
All are different. Greece, and Greece alone, had the power,
or seemed to have the power, to fuse them; receding from
the magic centre the fibres quiver, impotently aware.
Byron was nearer to his goal on the stony slopes of Parnassus
or in the dusty streets that bordered the Choragic Monument of Lysicrates than he ever was among the canals of
Venice or the busy highways of Rome. And he knew it.

I have said that Canto IV is the canto of splendours: of
these there is space here to point out only the major
brilliances. The Byronic spotlight falls on Venice (i–xviii);
Arqua (xxx–xxxii); Ferrara (xxxv–xxxix); Florence (xlviii–
lxi); the lake of Thrasimene (lxii); Terni (lxix–lxxii); and
Rome (lxxviii–clxxii). If this were a travelogue the achieve-
ment would be great enough, but for Byron the moment is
always 'this grace dissolved in place', and every place has its
distinct grace to inform it. Venice mediates a passionate
regret for vanished *power*, together with the charm of music,
architecture, and poetry which gave it meaning. Rome too
is power, but on a longer wavelength, as it were, of which
now we can pick up only certain frequencies: empire,
civilization, brutality, vastness, austerity (lxxviii, lxxx,
cxxxix, cxxviii, cxlvi), and the rest drifts back into the

eddies of time. Only in Byron do we have this sense of the *escaping* past, of meaning to be salvaged. Of the past *as* meaning, of wisdom on its way to extinction; of the irreplaceable historic legacy.

Between the spotlights come the moments of reflection. Canto II, with which we must constantly compare this canto, had no need of such moments; in Greece the reflective moment is one with the parched hillside and the fallen or slanting column. Man, history, philosophy are reduced to their correlatives: we live the present with the past (and the non-existent future, if you insist) through the worn sun-warm stone and the scent of thyme and the violent sunbeam and the wash of Odyssean seas. There is little reflection in Canto II. Canto IV, with all its grandeur of crumbling wall and *European* history (I underline the adjective to distinguish *this* history from that other history which fits into a metaphysical pattern stretching out to India on the one hand and Druidic Britain on the other) lacks this dimension, and makes up for it by a complicated interweaving of incident, description, reflection and personal emotion. Byron was more himself, more truly 'personal', when he threw his reactions into the extrovert violence of *The Giaour* and *The Corsair*, than when he reflected among the ruins of the Coliseum or on the shores of Thrasimene. For while I am sure Goethe was quite off the beam when he remarked of Byron that 'When he reflects, he is a child', meaning apparently that Byron is the poet of passion and its attendant action, he was right in seeing that Byron was not a poet peddling *his* sort of reflection: not at all a poet of concepts or formulations, or of the isolation of an idea from its context, of word-textures offered as substitutes for life-textures.

IV. ORIENTAL AND OTHER TALES

Between the first two and the last two cantos of *Childe Harold* came the narrative poems on Middle Eastern themes that I shall call the Oriental Tales: *The Giaour* (1813), *The Bride of Abydos* (1813), *The Corsair* (1814), *Lara* (1814), *The Siege of Corinth* (1816). They were followed by three more Tales which are not linked to the Eastern scene: *The Prisoner of Chillon* (1816), *Parisina* (1816), and *Mazeppa* (1819). They are all extrapolations ('statements in other terms') of what we might call the energic component of Byron which could not find expression in the meditative structures of Cantos II and IV. For Byron, poetry is basically a projection, the verbal sloughing off of what cannot be put into action; yet such a projection can itself be a new life-form, a creation existing alongside the poet, as it were (cf. *Childe Harold* III, vi). These Tales embody a 'romantic' element which Byron sensed had to be eliminated before he could pass on to the 'metaphysics' (his own word) of Canto III and the 'hypostatics' (my word, meaning a fusion of human and non-human *personae*) of Canto IV.

In the Tales we are in Nietzsche's world, not Spinoza's: here power is law, and the satisfaction of passion brushes every other consideration aside. The surface effect is melodrama. As characters, the *dramatis personae* of these Tales can hardly be said to exist, and the plots are absurdly simplified. Yet the total effect is not negligible. All the Tales express obsession with the Fall; all the heroes are variations on Adam, Cain, the Scapegoat, the Wandering Jew. In these melodramas 'The wandering outlaw of his own dark mind' works out his complex destiny. Freedom is the apple with which Gulnare tempts Conrad in *The Corsair*; in *Lara* the guilty pair are exiled from their eastern Eden. The Cain-Abel drama is re-enacted in the murder of Ezzelin. A Fall-Redemption pattern links all the Tales, though it is inconclusive: we may see it as bliss-danger-disaster-rescue-counterperil, Byron's 'cynicism' rejecting a happy ending. And though all these dramas except *Lara* are sited in the Greek scene (and even *Lara* is related to it), we miss certain of the resonances of *Childe Harold*, what I might call the eternity-dimension: the stars no longer twinkle through the loops of time. We are given brilliant and indeed moving descriptions of landscape and seascape, but these are emotionally unrelated to the human action, which is seen as incompatible with the spirit of its setting (*The Giaour*, lines 46–67). These 'Edens of the eastern wave' have been desecrated by human guilt, and the gates to their enjoyment are closed, 'With dreadful faces thronged and fiery arms', in Milton's phrase. The ethos of *Paradise Lost* is pervasively present, curiously combined with that of Dante—'that gentleness in Dante beyond all gentleness', as he perceptively notes in his Journal for 29 January 1821—'who *but* Dante could have introduced any 'gentleness' at all into *Hell*?' Here too, in the Tales, are adumbrations of those Dantesque circles, 'bolges', whirlpools of narrowing and deepening guilt, which are to constitute the very structure of *Don Juan*. That the fiery vortex is the basic Byronic ideogram is a point I have already made: in a celebrated passage of *The Giaour* which is strikingly similar to section IV of 'Little Gidding', the 'whirling gulf of phantasy and flame' of *Childe Harold* III, vii is the prison of the scorpion, Remorse:

> The Mind, that broods o'er guilty woes,
>   Is like the Scorpion girt by fire,
> In circle narrowing as it glows,
> The flames around their captive close,
> Till inly search'd by thousand throes,
>   And maddening in her ire,
> One sad and sole relief she knows,
> The sting she nourish'd for her foes,
> Whose venom never yet was vain,
> Gives but one pang, and cures all pain,
> And darts into her desperate brain . . .   (422-32)

A suicide-motif is here, and in the rest of the Tales, superimposed on the *weltschmerz* lamentation which runs through *Childe Harold*. Reading the Tales simply as narrative, it is not always easy to appreciate, unless on this supposition, the fatality which drives the Byronic hero to cast away

what the situation offers of simple love and goodness. Of
course there are classical pressures active too: the idea of
hubris, of a happiness coveted by mortals but beyond their
reach, frowned on by the gods.

> With shivering hearts the strife we saw
> Of passion with eternal law . . .

One finds one's thoughts returning to Matthew Arnold's
brilliant assessment. Law and passion are indeed the poles
around which the action of these Tales gyrates, antitheses
established by a variety of rhetorical devices. The first of
course is the sea-symbolism: storm / tide: passion / law. The
interpenetration of sea and land had been gentle in Canto II
of *Childe Harold*, the music of the Mediterranean's miniature
tides flowing into quiet coves, but in *The Giaour* a fiercer
harmony begins. The opening is calm, but it is the calm of
death:

> No breath of air to break the wave
> That rolls below the Athenian's grave . . .

This death-like slumber of Greece under her oppressor is
broken, within the limited circuit of *The Giaour*, by formidable storm-rhythms projected into the *human* action of the
poem:

> Who thundering comes on blackest steed,
> With slacken'd bit and hoof of speed?
> Beneath the clattering iron's sound
> The cavern'd echoes wake around
> In lash for lash, and bound for bound;
> The foam that streaks the courser's side
> Seems gather'd from the ocean-tide . . .   (180-6)

Indeed we must note, in the Tales, how little the sea-values
are presented in their own right (contrast *Childe Harold* and
Don Juan): these narratives are obsessive presentations of
certain 'romantic' aspects of the human dilemma, and Byron
is going to allow no tincture of the 'picturesque' to blunt
their existential impact.

This remains a constant. The Tales attracted, and still attract, by their authenticity. However brilliant the colours, however *outré* the action, however unbridled the passions, Byron is able to convince his readers that what he is writing about is what he himself has seen and experienced. No wonder that Walter Scott's verse romances, located most of them in an idealized Middle Ages, and lacking the note of passion, declined in popularity. This note of immediacy is struck in the first of the Tales, *The Giaour*, where the nub of the plot, the drowning of the Turkish girl, derives from a real life episode in which Byron was directly involved. (He did in fact save the girl from the fate she suffers in the poem: 'To describe the *feelings* of *that situation* were impossible—it is *icy* even to recollect them', he wrote in his diary some three years later.) This is Byron the man of action, a role in which he always preferred to see himself.

The plot of *The Giaour* is not easy to follow. Byron uses a deliberately cinematic technique, involving flashbacks in time and close-ups in focusing. And 'this snake of a poem', as he calls it himself, is the end-result of an interminable succession of afterthoughts, revisions and additions. Within the narrative itself we have to be alert to who is the narrator: sometimes Byron himself, commenting and moralizing, sometimes an old Turkish fisherman, presenting his very unsympathetic point of view; and finally, towards the close, the Giaour's own voice or that of the monk with whom he is speaking. The poem is an experiment, and a not wholly successful one; it is a collection of fragments, but these fragments are the foundation stones of all the later Tales— the foundations, and the germs, and as 'germs' presenting a concentration of Byronic essences which make the later narratives seem a little diluted, a little watered down. I wish I had space to linger over the great moments of the poem: the scorpion passage which I have already touched upon, the lyrical description of the Greek islands (to receive an even more powerful apotheosis in the Haidee episode of *Don Juan* and its attendant song, 'The isles of Greece'); the

meditation on death beginning 'He who hath bent him o'er
the dead' (lines 68-91); the great celebration of liberty
beginning 'Clime of the unforgotten brave!' (lines 103-41);
and, in an entirely different mood from these (Byron's
endless versatility!) the sombre meditations of

> The steed is vanish'd from the stall;
> No serf is seen in Hassan's hall;
> The lonely Spider's thin gray pall
> Waves slowly widening o'er the wall;
> The Bat builds in his Haram bower
> And in the fortress of his power
> The Owl usurps the beacon-tower ... (288-94)

and of

> A turban carved in coarsest stone,
> A pillar with rank weeds o'ergrown,
> Whereon can now be scarcely read
> The Koran verse that mourns the dead ... (723-6)

This has always seemed to me one of the most marvellous
of Byronic visualizations, catching as it does, without
rhetoric, this facet of Islam which, while remaining purely
Islamic, can say something to the traveller of another faith
and culture. From his letters too we understand the depth
of Byron's feelings for the cypress-circled Turkish grave-
yards: places of slanting, turban-topped tombstones which
seem uncared for but are never allowed to run to waste,
where the hemlock reaches to the height of the turban and
the cedar bends down to touch it too, and both are kept in
bounds by an intervention which is never seen but is
constantly (or perhaps sporadically) active. Who can tell?
I think Byron liked this feeling of a human activity which
was indistinguishable from the slow processes of nature.
And the sadness, sadness of Islam, the grey endurance among
the ceramic splendours, the acceptance of something less
than in the West would be considered a destiny: this too
passes into the Tales and modulates the brightness of the
Greek scene. Here again we are close to the Eliot of *Four
Quartets*, turning

behind the pig-sty to the dull façade
And the tombstone. And what you thought you came for
Is only a shell, a husk of meaning . . . (*Little Gidding*, I)

The sense of *spent* force, of an action which has been caught up into time, which crumbles, is ineffective, whose ineffectiveness is its essence, is conveyed in the later addition 'The browsing camels' bells are tinkling', and of course points forward to Tennyson and *The Lady of Shalott*: we meet it again in 'Little Gidding' II:

Ash on an old man's sleeve
Is all the ash the burnt roses leave.
Dust in the air suspended
Marks the place where a story ended . . .

and it is Yeats's finale too:

An old house
Where nothing stirs but a mouse.

Ultimately, this indoor world (for the grave too is indoors) is not Byron's world. He touches it, from time to time, and I think he might have touched it more but for his mother and all the dreadful memories of his youth; *they* drove him outwards, denied him a focus, made him dilate himself where his pressing need was for concentration.

Each Tale is a new metrical experiment, and *The Bride of Abydos* opens with a tidal surge of anapaests which demonstrate that this measure can be as languorous in one context as it can be vigorous in another ('The Destruction of Sennacherib' for instance). Later sections give us Coleridgean deviations from the strict octosyllabic couplet—interlaced rhymes, expanded lines, a wealth of triplets. The action is more close-knit than *The Giaour*'s, and better-sustained: the dominant Fall theme, overtly presented in the pentameters of section VI (Byron's sense of decorum leads him to drop the octosyllabics)—

> Fair, as the first that fell of womankind,
>   When on that dread yet lovely serpent smiling,
> Whose image then was stamp'd upon her mind —
>   But once beguil'd — and ever more beguiling . . . (158-61)

—provides the ground-note of the poem. The sea is feminine
here, seductive and betraying, though the betrayal is unconscious. The hero, Selim, is androgynous, a pawn almost
in the fierce subterranean battle between Zuleika and
Giaffir. There is an inner-looking, enclosed feeling to the
poem which is quite absent from *The Giaour*, a sense of
intrigue and stifled passion, a Harem atmosphere which
oppresses, but gives Byron the opportunity to demonstrate
that his gift for interior description is not inferior to his
genius for landscape:

> And by her comboloio[1] lies
> A Koran of illumined dyes;
> And many a bright emblazon'd rhyme
> By Persian scribes redeem'd from time;
> And o'er those scrolls, not oft so mute,
> Reclines her now neglected lute;
> And round her lamp of fretted gold
> Bloom flowers in urns of China's mould;
> The richest work of Iran's loom,
> And Sheeraz' tribute of perfume;
> All that can eye or sense delight
>   Are gather'd in that gorgeous room.
>   But yet it hath an air of gloom.
> She, of this Peri cell the sprite,
> What doth she hence, and on so rude a night?   (II, v)

What this passage owes to *Christabel* it repays, and in full
measure, in its contributions to 'The Eve of St Agnes' and
'The Eve of St Mark', and beyond them to Morris and
Tennyson.

[1] A bracelet of amber beads.

The Corsair (1814) returns us to the outdoor world of *The Giaour*, but with a difference. The poem was begun and completed in the last fortnight of December 1813, an extraordinary feat of composition. The 'difference' resides in the growing importance of the feminine element, which Byron now begins to weave contrapuntally, rather than antiphonally (if I may so express it) with the masculine. *The Giaour* was a Tale in which the hero had failed to rescue the heroine; in *The Bride* the heroine causes the death of the hero. In *The Corsair* the heroine rescues the hero, but does so in such a way as to destroy his honour. In *The Giaour* the landscape dominates the human pair, in *The Bride* heroic landscape is balanced by seductive interior, in *The Corsair* there is an interpenetration of feminine 'interiority' with the outdoor masculine scene. This is beautifully conveyed in the diptych of the setting sun and rising moon which opens Canto III. This passage is borrowed—'I scarce know why', Byron said—from the as yet unpublished 'The Curse of Minerva', and it fits much better here: indeed, it is possible to see *The Corsair* as a transposition into narrative terms of the sun-moon counterpoint of this splendid passage, which impresses by its immediacy ('written on the spot, in the Spring of 1811', as Byron notes). It also affords us a glimpse into the workings of Byron's mind, from landscape into life and from life back again into landscape. Here was something Byron had felt so deeply that it had become a part of his being and had to be re-expressed in lyric, in narrative, and in dramatic terms at each new stimulus. Who, he asks, can ever forget the magic of Greece?:

> Not he—whose heart nor time nor distance frees,
> Spell-bound within the clustering Cyclades!
>
> (*The Corsair*, III, ii)

To this extent—and it is wide enough—we may see the Oriental Tales as the extrovert rendering of Byron's long love-affair with Greece. They are also the extroversion of the

fire element in Byron, providing a vent for the aggressive
and passionate stresses which could not be fused into the
melancholy, meditative earth-and-air pattern of Canto II
of *Childe Harold*.

I have suggested that the Tales are variations on the
theme of peril, disaster, rescue, counter-disaster. In *The
Corsair* Conrad is captured in rescuing Gulnare, and is then
rescued by Gulnare at the price of honour. The counter-
disaster comes in *Lara* (1814) which is the sequel to *The
Corsair*: a sombre, somewhat featureless and obsessively
guilt-racked narrative which takes us away from the
Mediterranean scene (Lara, the former Corsair, returns to
his ancestral home, apparently in some inland region of
Spain) and thus from the sea; in so doing the poem forfeits
a dimension and a resonance which the other Tales had
possessed. We miss the sea voices. It is the most complex of
the Tales, and the most obscure. As counter-disaster, it fuses
certain features of *The Corsair*: Medora, Conrad's 'pure'
love, interacts with the 'guilty' Gulnare to evolve the
'page-boy' Kaled; Gulnare's treachery enters Conrad's soul
to render him capable of the assassination of Ezzelin (who
himself has a mysterious relationship with Medora). The
main interest of the Tale lies in its elaboration of the Byronic
hero. But this I must leave for discussion in a later essay.

Between *Lara* and the rest of the Tales came the *Hebrew
Melodies* (1815). These are reflective lyrics which I shall
discuss in my second essay, but they had their influence on
the sequence of the Tales. They are boldly experimental in
their manipulation of poetic forms and metres, and the
possibilities here explored are exploited in the next of the
Tales, *The Siege of Corinth* (Jan. 1816). We are listening
to a new music, which has learned much from *Christabel*
and 'Kubla Khan' yet preserves its own masculine drive and
stress. We return to the tetrameter, but a tetrameter infinitely more flexible than that of *The Giaour*. The sea too
returns:

'Tis midnight: on the mountains brown
The cold, round moon shines deeply down;
Blue roll the waters, blue the sky
Spreads like an ocean hung on high . . .
The waves on either shore lay there
Calm, clear and azure as the air;
And scarce their foam the pebbles shook,
But murmur'd meekly as the brook.
The winds were pillow'd on the waves;
The banners droop'd along their staves,
And, as they fell around them furling,
Above them shone the crescent curling;
And that deep silence was unbroke,
Save where the watch his signal spoke,
Save where the steed neigh'd oft and shrill,
And echo answer'd from the hill,
And the wide hum of that wild host
Rustled like leaves from coast to coast,
As rose the Muezzin's voice in air
In midnight call to wonted prayer . . . (xi)

Now sea responds to land in a harmony unheard before
in Byron's verse, in what one can only call a kind of com-
passion, a fellow-feeling which links man too with his dust:

The silent pillar, lone and grey,
Claim'd kindred with their sacred clay;
Their spirits wrapp'd the dusky mountain,
Their memory sparkled o'er the fountain;
The meanest rill, the mightiest river
Roll'd mingling with their fame for ever.
Despite of every yoke she bears,
The land is glory's still and theirs!
'Tis still a watchword to the earth:
When man would do a deed of worth
He points to Greece, and turns to tread,
So sanction'd, on the tyrant's head:
He looks to her, and rushes on
Where life is lost, or freedom won.   (xv)

The later narratives—*Parisina, The Prisoner of Chillon,
Mazeppa*, seem to me less successful. Divorced from Greece,
indeed from the classical scene in general, they have
lost a nerve, a dimension; here Byron's weaknesses show
themselves without his strength—sentimentality, melodrama, frigidity, and occasionally bombast. *Parisina* (1816)
was published along with *The Siege of Corinth*; the
reviewers attacked it on moral grounds ('the guilty passion
of a bastard son for his father's wife') while our *caveats* are
likely to be otherwise directed: the insipidity of the heroine,
the supineness of the hero, and indeed the whole unreality
of a situation which could hardly arise nowadays. The
versification is in no ways any advance on the earlier Tales.
The Prisoner of Chillon is in another category: here Byron
was fired by direct access, and in company with Shelley
(who always brought out the best in Byron), to the scene
he was writing of: the result is a very superior tear-jerker,
but could one say more for it than that? There are great
lines, certainly:

>   . . . to bend
> Once more, upon the mountains high,
> The quiet of a loving eye   (330–1)

and

> With spiders I had friendship made,
> And watch'd them in their sullen trade,
> Had seen the mice by moonlight play,
> And why should I feel less than they?   (381–4)

but to gauge the remoteness of all this from the multi-
dimensioned world of the Oriental Tales we have only to
remember

> The steed is vanish'd from the stall;
> No serf is seen in Hassan's hall;
> The lonely Spider's thin gray pall

Waves slowly widening o'er the wall;[1]
The Bat builds in his Haram bower
And in the fortress of his power
The Owl usurps the beacon-tower . . . (*Giaour*, 288-94)

The 'Sonnet on Chillon' (in spite of Byron's dislike of the form, one of the supreme sonnets of our language) distils in its fourteen lines the essence of *The Prisoner*'s fourteen strophes.

Mazeppa, finally, extracts the extrovert maximum from all these stories. Let us note that in them the masculine energy, supreme in *The Giaour*, has been steadily subordinated to the feminine. *Parisina* is an almost complete emasculation. In *The Prisoner of Chillon* the hero is submerged *beneath* the lake in a sealed dungeon, a passive sufferer watching his brothers die as the Ancient Mariner had watched his shipmates, and at length shrinking from deliverance. Dante's Ugolino and the Mariner meet in Byron's Bonnivard. In *Mazeppa* there are other resonances, chiefly from 'Kubla Khan'; but there is no imitation—Byron's uncanny power of assimilating the essence of another mind's 'message' and transposing it into his own ideograms was never more convincingly at work. Here 'the royal madman' Charles XII is the Khan, to whom 'ancestral voices prophesying war' sound together with 'the mingled measure' of Mazeppa's narrative, while Coleridge's 'woman wailing for her demon lover' is evoked by 'the first moonrise of midnight' shining on the mad passion of Theresa and Mazeppa; and the Abyssinian maid finds her counterpart in the Cossack maid, who in her gentleness befriends the exhausted hetman. The frenzied gallop of the wild horse through a wolf-infested wilderness recalls the turbulent passage of the river Alph through the 'caverns measureless to man' of 'Kubla Khan': both are emblems of unconscious, instinctual forces.

[1] Cf. T. S. Eliot's 'East Coker' I, 9-13, and 'Little Gidding' II. The phrases, images and rhythms of Byron's Oriental Tales are pervasively present in *Four Quartets*.

The wild horse (which since Freud we have come to recognize as a blatant sexual symbol) acts as the medium between the hero's sense of guilt and his impulse towards self-punishment; yet Mazeppa is saved by this same energy, though not released—liberation is achieved only through the innocent tenderness of the Cossack maid. *Mazeppa* is *The Corsair*'s mirror-image, a transposition of action into suffering. And it is the Mercator's projection of 'Kubla Khan', Coleridge's vertical and vortical patterns being flattened out, as it were, into a linear, horizontal diagram which shows nevertheless the same love / war and action / suffering contours. Byron, with the rapid glance of genius, has divined the interiority of 'Kubla Khan', the 'meaning' over which critics have been quarrelling for a century and a half, and his exegesis is *Mazeppa*. Whatever we may think of the success of Byron's experiments in psychological narrative in the Tales, we ought to abandon once for all the notion that they can be dismissed as trivia.

BYRON

A Select Bibliography

(Place of publication London, unless stated otherwise. Detailed bibliographical information will also be found in the appropriate volume of
The Cambridge Bibliography of English Literature and *The Oxford History
of English Literature*.)

Bibliography:

THE LIFE OF LORD BYRON, by Hon. R. Noel (1890)
—includes *Bibliography* by J. P. Anderson, containing extensive lists
of magazine articles about Byron and of musical settings.

A BIBLIOGRAPHY OF SUCCESSIVE EDITIONS AND TRANSLATIONS in *The
Works of Lord Byron. Poetry*, Vol. VII (1904), ed. E. H. Coleridge
—the best general bibliography of the poems.

BYRON IN ENGLAND, by S. C. Chew (1924)
—contains an extensive list of Byroniana.

BIBLIOGRAPHICAL CATALOGUE of the First Editions, Proof Copies and
Manuscripts of Books by Lord Byron. Exhibited at the First
Edition Club, January 1925 (1925).

A DESCRIPTIVE CATALOGUE OF . . . MANUSCRIPTS AND FIRST EDITIONS . . .
AT THE UNIVERSITY OF TEXAS, ed. R. H. Griffith and H. M. Jones;
Austin, Texas (1924).

BYRON AND BYRONIANA. A Catalogue of Books (1930)
—an important sale catalogue, valuable for reference, issued by Elkin
Mathews, the London booksellers.

A BIBLIOGRAPHY OF THE WRITINGS IN VERSE AND PROSE OF GEORGE
GORDON NOEL, BARON BYRON. With Letters illustrating his Life and
Work and particularly his attitude towards Keats, by T. J. Wise,
2 vols (1932-3)
—the standard technical bibliography. Incorporates the material of
the same author's *A Byron Library*, 1928, the privately printed
catalogue of the Byron Collection in the Ashley Library, now in
the British Museum.

THE ROE-BYRON COLLECTION, Newstead Abbey; Nottingham (1937)
—the catalogue of the collection at Byron's ancestral home.

Note: The archives of John Murray, Byron's publishers, at 50
Albemarle Street, London, contain important manuscript material.

Collected Works:

THE POETICAL WORKS, 2 vols; Philadelphia (1813)

—the first collected edition, followed throughout the nineteenth
century by numerous other collected editions in several volumes,
published in London, Paris, New York, and elsewhere.

THE WORKS, 4 vols (1815)

—new editions, 1818-20 (8 vols); 1825 (8 vols); 1831 (6 vols).

THE WORKS, with His Letters and Journals, and His Life, by Thomas
Moore, ed. J. Wright, 17 vols (1832-3).

THE POETICAL WORKS. New Edition, with the Text Carefully Revised,
6 vols (1857).

THE POETICAL WORKS, edited, with a Critical Memoir by W. M.
Rossetti. Illustrated by Ford Madox Brown, 8 vols (1870).

THE WORKS. A New, Revised, and Enlarged Edition with Illustrations,
including Portraits, 13 vols (1898-1904)

—*Poetry*, ed. E. H. Coleridge, 7 vols; *Letters and Journals*, ed. R. H.
Prothero, 6 vols.

THE POETICAL WORKS. The Only Complete and Copyright Text in
one volume. Edited with a Memoir, by E. H. Coleridge (1905)

—the standard edition, often reprinted.

Selections:

A SELECTION FROM THE WORK OF LORD BYRON, edited and prefaced by
A. C. Swinburne (1866).

POETRY OF BYRON, chosen and arranged by M. Arnold (1881).

POEMS, ed. H. J. C. Grierson (1923).

THE SHORTER BYRON . . . , chosen and edited by E. Rhys (1927).

THE BEST OF BYRON, ed. R. A. Rice; New York (1933).

DON JUAN AND OTHER SATIRIC POEMS, ed. L. I. Bredvold; New York
(1935).

CHILDE HAROLD'S PILGRIMAGE AND OTHER ROMANTIC POEMS, ed. S. C.
Chew (1936).

SATIRICAL AND CRITICAL POEMS, ed. J. Bennett; Cambridge (1937).

BYRON, POETRY AND PROSE. With essays by Scott, Hazlitt, Macaulay,
etc. With an introduction by Sir A. Quiller-Couch and notes by
D. Nichol Smith (1940).

SELECTIONS FROM POETRY, LETTERS AND JOURNALS, ed. P. Quennell
(1949).

Separate Works:

FUGITIVE PIECES [Newark, 1806]

—privately printed and anonymous. Facsimile reprint, ed. H. B. Forman, 1886.

POEMS ON VARIOUS OCCASIONS; Newark (1807)

—privately printed and anonymous.

HOURS OF IDLENESS: A Series of Poems Original and Translated; Newark (1807).

POEMS ORIGINAL AND TRANSLATED; second ed. of *Hours of Idleness*; Newark (1808)

—contains five new pieces.

ENGLISH BARDS AND SCOTCH REVIEWERS: A Satire [1809]

—the early editions of this poem were frequently counterfeited.

ADDRESS WRITTEN BY LORD BYRON. The Genuine Rejected Addresses, Presented to the Committee of Management for Drury Lane Theatre: Preceded by that written by Lord Byron and adopted by the Committee (1812).

CHILDE HAROLD'S PILGRIMAGE: A Romaunt. Cantos I and II (1812); Canto III (1816); Canto IV (1818); Cantos I-IV were collected in 2 vols (1819).

THE CURSE OF MINERVA: A Poem (1812).

WALTZ: An Apostrophic Hymn 'by Horace Hornem, Esq.' (1813).

THE GIAOUR: A Fragment of a Turkish Tale (1813).

THE BRIDE OF ABYDOS: A Turkish Tale (1813).

THE CORSAIR: A Tale (1814).

ODE TO NAPOLEON BUONAPARTE, [Anon] (1814).

LARA: A Tale (1814).

HEBREW MELODIES, Ancient and Modern with appropriate Symphonies and Accompaniments (1815).

THE SIEGE OF CORINTH: A Poem. PARISINA: A Poem, [Anon] (1816).

[POEMS ON HIS DOMESTIC CIRCUMSTANCES] (i. Fare Thee Well. ii. A Sketch from Private Life) (1816)

—these two poems had been privately printed and separately printed in the same year. Various editions of this collection with additional poems were published in 1816.

POEMS (1816).

THE PRISONER OF CHILLON AND OTHER POEMS (1816).

MONODY ON THE DEATH OF THE RIGHT HON. R. B. SHERIDAN. Written at the Request of a Friend, to be Spoken at Drury Lane (1816).

THE LAMENT OF TASSO (1817).

MANFRED: A Dramatic Poem (1817).

BEPPO: A Venetian Story (1818). Anonymous

—fourth ed., with additional stanzas, 1818.

MAZEPPA: A Poem (1819).

DON JUAN. Cantos I and II (1819); Cantos III, IV, V (1821); Cantos VI, VII, VIII (1823); Cantos IX, X, XI (1823); Cantos XII, XIII, XIV (1823); Cantos XV, XVI (1824) originally published anonymously.

—first collected edition, 2 vols, Edinburgh 1825; ed. T. G. Steffan and W. W. Pratt, 4 vols, Austin, Texas 1957; (the fullest edition, of which Vol. I contains a detailed study of the composition of the poem).

MARINO FALIERO, DOGE OF VENICE: An Historical Tragedy. THE PROPHECY OF DANTE: A Poem (1821).

SARDANAPALUS: A Tragedy. THE TWO FOSCARI: A Tragedy. CAIN: A Mystery (1821).

THE VISION OF JUDGMENT (1822)

—a product of Byron's feud with Southey, first printed in *The Liberal*, 1822, an ephemeral paper promoted by Byron and Leigh Hunt. Published as *The Two Visions* with Southey's 'Vision of Judgment' in the same year.

HEAVEN AND EARTH: A Mystery, [Anon[(1823).

—first printed in *The Liberal*, 1823.

THE AGE OF BRONZE: Or, Carmen Seculare et Annus haud Mirabilis, [Anon[(1823).

THE ISLAND: Or, Christian and His Comrades (1823).

WERNER: A Tragedy (1823).

THE PARLIAMENTARY SPEECHES OF LORD BYRON. Printed from the Copies prepared by his Lordship for Publication (1824).

THE DEFORMED TRANSFORMED: A Drama (1824).

Diaries, Letters, etc.

LETTER TO [John Murray] ON THE REV. W. L. BOWLES' STRICTURES ON THE LIFE AND WRITINGS OF POPE (1821).

CORRESPONDENCE OF LORD BYRON WITH A FRIEND, including his Letters to his Mother in 1809-11, ed. A. R. C. Dallas, 3 vols; Paris (1825).

LETTERS AND JOURNALS OF LORD BYRON, with Notices of his Life, by T. Moore, 2 vols (1830, revised edition 1875).

LETTERS AND JOURNALS, ed. R. E. Prothero, 6 vols (1898-1904).

POEMS AND LETTERS, edited from the original MSS. in the possession of W. K. Bixby, by W. N. C. Carlton; privately printed, Chicago (1912).

LORD BYRON'S CORRESPONDENCE, chiefly with Lady Melbourne, Mr
Hobhouse, the Hon. Douglas Kinnaird, and P. B. Shelley, ed.
John Murray, 2 vols (1922).

SELECTED LETTERS, ed. V. H. Collins; Oxford (1928).

THE RAVENNA JOURNAL, mainly compiled at Ravenna in 1821, with
an Introduction by Lord Ernle [R. E. Prothero] (1928)
—printed for the members of the First Edition Club.

LETTERS, ed. R. G. Howarth with an Introduction by André Maurois
(1933).

BYRON LETTERS AND DIARIES: A SELF PORTRAIT, ed. P. Quennell, 2 vols
(1950)
—the largest and best selection of Byron's correspondence, including
many hitherto unpublished letters.

BYRON: HIS VERY SELF AND VOICE, ed. E. J. Lovell (1954)
—a collection of Byron's conversation.

Some Critical and Biographical Studies:

A JOURNEY THROUGH ALBANIA AND OTHER PROVINCES OF TURKEY, by
J. C. Hobhouse (1813).

HISTORY OF A SIX WEEKS' TOUR, by P. B. Shelley (1817).

MEMOIRS OF THE LIFE AND WRITINGS OF THE RT. HON. LORD BYRON, with
Anecdotes of Some of his Contemporaries, by [J. Watkins] (1822).

JOURNAL OF THE CONVERSATIONS OF LORD BYRON: Noted during a
Residence with his Lordship at Pisa, in the Years 1821 and 1822,
by T. Medwin (1824).

NOTES ON CAPTAIN MEDWIN'S CONVERSATIONS OF LORD BYRON, by
John Murray; privately printed (1824)
—reprinted in *Works*, 1829.

RECOLLECTIONS OF THE LIFE OF LORD BYRON, from the Year 1808 to the
End of 1814, by R. C. Dallas (1824).

THE SPIRIT OF THE AGE, by W. Hazlitt (1825)
—contains an essay on Byron.

A NARRATIVE OF LORD BYRON'S LAST JOURNEY TO GREECE, by Count P.
Gamba (1825).

ANECDOTES OF LORD BYRON FROM AUTHENTIC SOURCES, by [Alexander
Kilgour] (1825).

THE LAST DAYS OF LORD BYRON: With his Lordship's Opinions on
Various Subjects, particularly on the State and Prospects of Greece,
by Major W. Parry (1825).

NARRATIVE OF A SECOND VISIT TO GREECE, including Facts connected with the Last Days of Lord Byron, Extracts from Correspondence, Official Documents, etc., ed. Edward Blaquiere (1825).

THE LIFE, WRITINGS, OPINIONS AND TIMES OF THE RT. HON. GEORGE GORDON NOEL BYRON, LORD BYRON, by an English Gentleman in the Greek Military Service, and Comrade of his Lordship. Compiled from Authentic Documents and from Long Personal Acquaintance, 3 vols (1825)

—ascribed to the publisher, Matthew Iley.

LORD BYRON AND SOME OF HIS CONTEMPORARIES, by Leigh Hunt (1828).

THE LIFE OF LORD BYRON, by J. Galt (1830).

CONVERSATIONS ON RELIGION WITH LORD BYRON AND OTHERS, by J. Kennedy (1830).

MEMOIRS OF THE AFFAIRS OF GREECE, with Various Anecdotes Relating to Lord Byron, and an Account of his Last Illness and Death, by J. Millingen (1831).

CONVERSATIONS OF LORD BYRON WITH THE COUNTESS OF BLESSINGTON, by Marguerite Gardiner, Countess of Blessington (1834).

CRITICAL AND HISTORIC ESSAYS, by T. B. Macaulay (1842)

—includes review of *Letters and Journals of Lord Byron; with Notices of his Life*, by T. Moore, 1830.

LECTURES ON THE ENGLISH POETS, by W. Hazlitt (1858).

RECOLLECTIONS OF THE LAST DAYS OF SHELLEY AND BYRON, by E. J. Trelawny (1858; ed. E. Dowden, 1906)

—see also the same author's *Records of Shelley, Byron, and the Author*, 2 vols, 1878, new eds. 1887, 1905.

LORD BYRON JUGÉ PAR LES TÉMOINS DE SA VIE, by Countess T. Guiccioli, 2 vols (1868)

—English translation, 1869.

MEDORA LEIGH: A History and An Autobiography, by E. M. Leigh, ed. C. Mackay (1869).

A CONTEMPORARY ACCOUNT OF THE SEPARATION OF LORD AND LADY BYRON: Also of the Destruction of Lord Byron's Memoirs, by J. C. Hobhouse; privately printed (1870)

—reprinted in Hobhouse's *Recollections of a Long Life*.

BYRON, by J. Nichol (1880)

—in the *English Men of Letters* series.

THE REAL LORD BYRON: New Views of the Poet's Life, by J. C. Jeaffreson, 2 vols (1883).

BYRON RE-STUDIED IN HIS DRAMAS. An Essay, by W. Gerard [Smith] (1886).

'Byron', by M. Arnold, *Essays in Criticism*, 2nd series (1888).

THE LIFE OF LORD BYRON, by the Hon. R. Noel (1890).

LAST LINKS WITH BYRON, SHELLEY AND KEATS, by W. Graham (1898).

JOURNAL OF EDWARD ELLERKER WILLIAMS, Companion of Shelley and Byron in 1821 and 1822. With an Introduction by R. Garnett (1902).

ASTARTE: A Fragment of Truth concerning Lord Byron, by Ralph Milbanke, Earl of Lovelace; privately printed (1905)

—enlarged edition, published 1921.

LORD BYRON AND HIS DETRACTORS. *Astarte. Lord Byron and Lord Lovelace*, by Sir J. Murray; *Lord Lovelace on the Separation of Lord and Lady Byron*, by R. E. Prothero (1906)

—privately printed for members of the Roxburghe Club.

BYRON: THE LAST PHASE, by R. J. F. Edgcumbe (1909).

RECOLLECTIONS OF A LONG LIFE, by J. C. Hobhouse (1909-11).

THE DIARY OF DR JOHN WILLIAM POLIDORI, relating to Byron, etc.

—edited and elucidated by W. M. Rossetti (1911).

LORD BYRON AS A SATIRIST IN VERSE, by C. M. Fuess (1912).

BYRON, by E. Colburn Mayne, 2 vols (1912, new ed. 1924)

—see also the same author's *The Life and Letters of Lady Noel Byron*, 1929.

LORD BYRON'S ILLNESS AND DEATH as described in a Letter to the Hon. Augusta Leigh, dated from Missolonghi April 20, 1824, by W. Fletcher; privately printed, Nottingham (1920).

THE RELATIONS OF LORD BYRON AND AUGUSTA LEIGH. With a Comparison of the Characters of Byron and Shelley. Four letters by E.J. Trelawny; privately printed (1920).

BYRON IN ENGLAND: His Fame and After Fame, by S. C. Chew (1924).

BYRON: THE LAST JOURNEY, April 1823-April 1824, by the Hon. Harold Nicolson (1924)

—new ed. 1948.

BYRON IN PERSPECTIVE, by J. D. Symon (1924).

BYRON, THE POET. A Centenary Volume, ed. W. A. Briscoe (1924)

—contains essays by Haldane, Grierson and others.

THE BACKGROUND OF ENGLISH LITERATURE, by H. J. C. Grierson (1925)

—contains 'Byron and English Society'.

LA FORTUNA DI BYRON IN INGHILTERRA, by M. Praz; Florence (1925)

—see also *The Romantic Agony*, translated A. Davidson, 1933.

ALLEGRA: The Story of Byron and Miss Clairmont, by A. C. Gordon; New York (1926).

THE HAUNTED CASTLE, by E. Railo (1927).

BYRON, ET LE BESOIN DE LA FATALITÉ, by C. Du Bos; Paris (1929)
—English translation by E. Colburn Mayne, 1932.

LORD BYRON: PERSÖNLICHKEIT UND WERK, by H. Richter (1929).

BYRON, by André Maurois, 2 vols; Paris (1930)
—English translation by H. Miles, 1930.

BYRON: THE YEARS OF FAME, by P. Quennell (1935).

ALLEGRA, by I. Origo (1935).

BYRON: ROMANTIC PARADOX, by W. J. Calvert (1935).

REVALUATION, by F. R. Leavis (1936)
—contains his influential essay 'Byron's Satire'.

FROM ANNE TO VICTORIA, ed. B. Dobrée (1937)
—contains 'Byron' by T. S. Eliot, reprinted in *On Poetry and Poets*, 1957.

BYRON AS SKEPTIC AND BELIEVER, by E. W. Marjarum; Princeton, N.J. (1938).

TO LORD BYRON: Feminine Profiles, Based upon Unpublished Letters 1807-1824, by G. Paston and P. Quennell (1939).

'Byron and the East: Literary Sources of the Turkish Tales', *Nineteenth Century Studies*, ed. H. Davies, W. C. de Vane and R. C. Bald (1940).

BYRON IN ITALY, by P. Quennell (1941).

BYRON'S DON JUAN, by E. F. Boyd (1945).

LORD BYRON'S FIRST PILGRIMAGE, by W. A. Borst; New Haven, Conn. (1948).

BYRON: THE RECORD OF A QUEST, by E. J. Lovell; Austin, Texas (1949).

THE LAST ATTACHMENT. The Story of Byron and Teresa Guiccioli, by I. Origo (1949).

GOETHE AND BYRON, by E. M. Butler (1951).

THE TRUE VOICE OF FEELING, by Sir H. Read (1951)
—contains an essay on Byron.

LORD BYRON, CHRISTIAN VIRTUES, by G. W. Knight (1952).

FAIR GREECE, SAD RELIC: Literary Philhellenism from Shakespeare to Byron, by T. Spencer (1954).

BYRON AND GOETHE, by E. M. Butler (1956).

LORD BYRON, UN TEMPÉRAMENT LITTÉRAIRE, by R. Escarpit; Paris (1956-7).

THE PELICAN GUIDE TO ENGLISH LITERATURE, Vol. V, ed. B. Ford (1957)
—contains 'Lord Byron', by J. D. Jump.

MAJOR ENGLISH ROMANTIC POETS, ed. C. D. Thorpe (1957)
—includes 'Irony and Image in Byron's Don Juan'.
BYRON, by L. A. Marchand, 3 vols (1957)
—the standard life.
THE METAMORPHOSES OF DON JUAN, by L. Weinstein (1959).
ON POETRY AND POETS, by T. S. Eliot (1959)
—contains an essay on Byron, first published in 1937.
BYRON AND THE SPOILER'S ART, by P. West (1960).
THE STYLE OF DON JUAN, by G. M. Ridenour; New Haven (1960)
—Yale Studies in English, Vol. CXLIV.
THE LATE LORD BYRON, by D. L. Moore (1961).
BYRON, by A. Rutherford (1961).
THE LOST TRAVELLERS, by B. Blackstone (1962)
—contains a chapter expanded from 'Guilt and Retribution in Byron's Sea Poems', in *A Review of English Literature*, Vol. II, January 1961.
LORD BYRON'S WIFE, by M. Elwin (1962).
THE BYRONIC HERO, by P. L. Thorster, Jr; Minnesota (1962).
THE STRUCTURE OF BYRON'S MAJOR POEMS, by W. J. Marshall; Philadelphia (1962).
BYRON: A Collection of Critical Essays, ed. P. West; Englewood Cliffs (1963).
BYRON THE POET, by M. K. Joseph (1964).
BYRON AND SHAKESPEARE, by G. Wilson Knight (1966).
FIERY DUST: BYRON'S POETIC DEVELOPMENT, by J. J. McGann; Chicago (1968).
THE JOURNALS OF CLAIRE CLAIRMONT, ed. M. K. Stocking; Cambridge, Mass. (1969).

Note: Reference should also be made to the following Nottingham Byron Foundation Lectures: *Byron's Lyrics*, by L. C. Martin (1948); *Byron and Switzerland*, by H. Straumann (1948); *Byron and Shelley*, by D. G. James (1951); *Byron's Dramatic Prose*, by G. Wilson Knight (1953); *Two Exiles: Lord Byron and D. H. Lawrence*, by G. Hough (1956; reprinted in *Image and Experience*, 1960); *Byron and Italy*, by G. Melchiori (1958); *Byron and the Greek Tradition*, by T. Spencer (1959); and *Byron's Dramas*, by B. Dobrée (1962).

WRITERS AND THEIR WORK

General Surveys:

THE DETECTIVE STORY IN BRITAIN:
Julian Symons

THE ENGLISH BIBLE: Donald Coggan

ENGLISH VERSE EPIGRAM:
G. Rostrevor Hamilton

ENGLISH HYMNS: A. Pollard

ENGLISH MARITIME WRITING:
Hakluyt to Cook: Oliver Warner

THE ENGLISH SHORT STORY I: & II:
T. O. Beachcroft

THE ENGLISH SONNET: P. Cruttwell

ENGLISH SERMONS: Arthur Pollard

ENGLISH TRAVELLERS IN THE
NEAR EAST: Robin Fedden

THREE WOMEN DIARISTS: M. Willy

Sixteenth Century and Earlier:

FRANCIS BACON: J. Max Patrick

BEAUMONT & FLETCHER: Ian Fletcher

CHAUCER: Nevill Coghill

RICHARD HOOKER: A. Pollard

THOMAS KYD: Philip Edwards

LANGLAND: Nevill Coghill

LYLY & PEELE: G. K. Hunter

MALORY: M. C. Bradbrook

MARLOWE: Philip Henderson

SIR THOMAS MORE: E. E. Reynolds

RALEGH: Agnes Latham

SIDNEY: Kenneth Muir

SKELTON: Peter Green

SPENSER: Rosemary Freeman

THREE 14TH-CENTURY ENGLISH
MYSTICS: Phyllis Hodgson

TWO SCOTS CHAUCERIANS:
H. Harvey Wood

WYATT: Sergio Baldi

Seventeenth Century:

SIR THOMAS BROWNE: Peter Green

BUNYAN: Henri Talon

CAVALIER POETS: Robin Skelton

CONGREVE: Bonamy Dobrée

DONNE: F. Kermode

DRYDEN: Bonamy Dobrée

ENGLISH DIARISTS:
Evelyn and Pepys: M. Willy

FARQUHAR: A. J. Farmer

JOHN FORD: Clifford Leech

GEORGE HERBERT: T. S. Eliot

HERRICK: John Press

HOBBES: T. E. Jessop

BEN JONSON: J. B. Bamborough

LOCKE: Maurice Cranston

ANDREW MARVELL: John Press

MILTON: E. M. W. Tillyard

RESTORATION COURT POETS:
V. de S. Pinto

SHAKESPEARE: C. J. Sisson

CHRONICLES: Clifford Leech

EARLY COMEDIES: Derek Traversi

LATER COMEDIES: G. K. Hunter

FINAL PLAYS: F. Kermode

HISTORIES: L. C. Knights

POEMS: F. T. Prince

PROBLEM PLAYS: Peter Ure

ROMAN PLAYS: T. J. B. Spencer

GREAT TRAGEDIES: Kenneth Muir

THREE METAPHYSICAL POETS:
Margaret Willy

IZAAK WALTON: Margaret Bottrall

WEBSTER: Ian Scott-Kilvert

WYCHERLEY: P. F. Vernon

Eighteenth Century:

BERKELEY: T. E. Jessop

BLAKE: Kathleen Raine

BOSWELL: P. A. W. Collins

BURKE: T. E. Utley

BURNS: David Daiches

WM. COLLINS: Oswald Doughty

COWPER: N. Nicholson

CRABBE: R. L. Brett

DEFOE: J. R. Sutherland

FIELDING: John Butt

GAY: Oliver Warner

GIBBON: C. V. Wedgwood

GOLDSMITH: A. Norman Jeffares

GRAY: R. W. Ketton-Cremer

HUME: Montgomery Belgion

JOHNSON: S. C. Roberts

POPE: Ian Jack

RICHARDSON: R. F. Brissenden

SHERIDAN: W. A. Darlington

CHRISTOPHER SMART: G. Grigson

SMOLLETT: Laurence Brander

STEELE, ADDISON: A. R. Humphreys

STERNE: D. W. Jefferson

SWIFT: J. Middleton Murry

SIR JOHN VANBRUGH: Bernard Harris

HORACE WALPOLE: Hugh Honour

Nineteenth Century:

MATTHEW ARNOLD: Kenneth Allott

JANE AUSTEN: S. Townsend Warner

BAGEHOT: N. St John-Stevas

THE BRONTË SISTERS: P. Bentley

BROWNING: John Bryson

E. B. BROWNING: Alethea Hayter

SAMUEL BUTLER: G. D. H. Cole

BYRON: Bernard Blackstone

CARLYLE: David Gascoyne

LEWIS CARROLL: Derek Hudson

CLOUGH: Isobel Armstrong
COLERIDGE: Kathleen Raine
CREEVEY & GREVILLE: J. Richardson
DE QUINCEY: Hugh Sykes Davies
DICKENS: K. J. Fielding
  EARLY NOVELS: T. Blount
  LATER NOVELS: B. Hardy
DISRAELI: Paul Bloomfield
GEORGE ELIOT: Lettice Cooper
FERRIER & GALT: W. M. Parker
FITZGERALD: Joanna Richardson
MRS GASKELL: Miriam Allott
GISSING: A. C. Ward
THOMAS HARDY: R. A. Scott-James
            and C. Day Lewis
HAZLITT: J. B. Priestley
HOOD: Laurence Brander
G. M. HOPKINS: Geoffrey Grigson
T. H. HUXLEY: William Irvine
KEATS: Edmund Blunden
LAMB: Edmund Blunden
LANDOR: G. Rostrevor Hamilton
EDWARD LEAR: Joanna Richardson
MACAULAY: G. R. Potter
MEREDITH: Phyllis Bartlett
JOHN STUART MILL: M. Cranston
WILLIAM MORRIS: P. Henderson
NEWMAN: J. M. Cameron
PATER: Iain Fletcher
PEACOCK: J. I. M. Stewart
ROSSETTI: Oswald Doughty
CHRISTINA ROSSETTI: G. Battiscombe
RUSKIN: Peter Quennell
SIR WALTER SCOTT: Ian Jack
SHELLEY: G. M. Matthews
SOUTHEY: Geoffrey Carnall
R. L. STEVENSON: G. B. Stern
SWINBURNE: H. J. C. Grierson
TENNYSON: F. L. Lucas
THACKERAY: Laurence Brander
FRANCIS THOMPSON: P. Butter
TROLLOPE: Hugh Sykes Davies
OSCAR WILDE: James Laver
WORDSWORTH: Helen Darbishire

Twentieth Century:

CHINUA ACHEBE: A. Ravenscroft
W. H. AUDEN: Richard Hoggart
HILAIRE BELLOC: Renée Haynes
ARNOLD BENNETT: F. Swinnerton
EDMUND BLUNDEN: Alec M. Hardie
ELIZABETH BOWEN: Jocelyn Brooke
ROBERT BRIDGES: J. Sparrow
ROY CAMPBELL: David Wright
JOYCE CARY: Walter Allen
G. K. CHESTERTON: C. Hollis
WINSTON CHURCHILL: John Connell
R. G. COLLINGWOOD: E.W.F. Tomlin
I. COMPTON-BURNETT: P. H. Johnson

JOSEPH CONRAD: Oliver Warner
WALTER DE LA MARE: K. Hopkins
NORMAN DOUGLAS: Ian Greenlees
T. S. ELIOT: M. C. Bradbrook
FIRBANK & BETJEMAN: J. Brooke
FORD MADOX FORD: Kenneth Young
E. M. FORSTER: Rex Warner
CHRISTOPHER FRY: Derek Stanford
JOHN GALSWORTHY: R. H. Mottram
WM. GOLDING: Clive Pemberton
ROBERT GRAVES: M. Seymour-Smith
GRAHAM GREENE: Francis Wyndham
L. P. HARTLEY & ANTHONY POWELL:
    P. Bloomfield and B. Bergonzi
A. E. HOUSMAN: Ian Scott-Kilvert
ALDOUS HUXLEY: Jocelyn Brooke
HENRY JAMES: Michael Swan
PAMELA HANSFORD JOHNSON:
                  Isabel Quigly
JAMES JOYCE: J. I. M. Stewart
RUDYARD KIPLING: Bonamy Dobrée
D. H. LAWRENCE: Kenneth Young
C. DAY LEWIS: Clifford Dyment
WYNDHAM LEWIS: E. W. F. Tomlin
COMPTON MACKENZIE: K. Young
LOUIS MACNEICE: John Press
KATHERINE MANSFIELD: Ian Gordon
JOHN MASEFIELD: L. A. G. Strong
SOMERSET MAUGHAM: J. Brophy
GEORGE MOORE: A. Norman Jeffares
EDWIN MUIR: J. C. Hall
J. MIDDLETON MURRY: Philip Mairet
SEAN O'CASEY: W. A. Armstrong
GEORGE ORWELL: Tom Hopkinson
POETS OF 1939-45 WAR: R. N. Currey
POWYS BROTHERS: R. C. Churchill
J. B. PRIESTLEY: Ivor Brown
HERBERT READ: Francis Berry
FOUR REALIST NOVELISTS: V. Brome
BERNARD SHAW: A. C. Ward
EDITH SITWELL: John Lehmann
OSBERT SITWELL: Roger Fulford
KENNETH SLESSOR: C. Semmler
C. P. SNOW: William Cooper
STRACHEY: R. A. Scott-James
SYNGE & LADY GREGORY: E. Coxhead
DYLAN THOMAS: G. S. Fraser
EDWARD THOMAS: Vernon Scannell
G. M. TREVELYAN: J. H. Plumb
WAR POETS: 1914-18: E. Blunden
EVELYN WAUGH: Christopher Hollis
H. G. WELLS: Montgomery Belgion
PATRICK WHITE: R. F. Brissenden
CHARLES WILLIAMS: J. Heath-Stubbs
ANGUS WILSON: K. W. Gransden
VIRGINIA WOOLF: B. Blackstone
W. B. YEATS: G. S. Fraser
ANDREW YOUNG & R. S. THOMAS:
    L. Clark and R. G. Thomas